Second Lieutenant Roland Mountfort, 1919

THE GREAT WAR LETTERS OF
ROLAND MOUNTFORT

Chris Holland and Rob Phillips

9 40.548142

Matador
5 Weir Road
Kibworth Beauchamp
Leicester LE8 0LQ, UK
Tel: (+44) 116 279 2299
Email: books@troubador.co.uk
Web: www.troubador.co.uk/matador

ISBN 978-1906510-794

A Cataloguing-in-Publication (CIP) catalogue record for this book
is available from the British Library.

Printed and bound in Great Britain by TJ International Ltd, Padstow, Cornwall

Matador is an imprint of Troubador Publishing Ltd

Contents

Maps

THE GREAT WAR LETTERS OF
ROLAND MOUNTFORT

PREFACE BY MALCOLM BROWN

Sometime in 1976, while reading a letter written sixty years earlier by a wounded soldier recuperating in hospital in London, I came across the following passage, describing just one sector of the battlefield of the Somme in early July 1916:

As far as you can see is a wilderness of torn up soil intersected with ruined trenches: it is like a man's face after small pox, or a telescopic view of the moon. The shell holes overlap & run into each other; some are mere scratches, some would house an average hay-stack; here and there a few distorted posts form all that remains of a wire entanglement. But the most striking feature is the debris that is lying, scattered on the surface & thick in the trenches. Lots of equipment, rifles, bayonets, shovels, shrapnel helmets, respirators, shell cases, iron posts, overcoats, ground sheets, bombs (in hundreds) – I don't suppose there is a square yard without some relic & reminder of the awful waste of war.

This still seems to me now, as it seemed to me then, a classic description worthy of being included in any anthology of modern quotations, and not merely one focused on the subject of battle and conflict. In a book I subsequently published under the title *Tommy Goes to War* I gave it pride of place in a special section entitled 'The Waste of War', borrowing that phrase, of course, from that description's final sentence. My publishers, Messrs J.M. Dent, were equally taken with it, so much so that they printed it in full on the reverse of the dust-jacket by way of an advertisement of the quality of the evidence the book contained. It must be added that this intended accolade somewhat misfired in that they had the quotation written out by hand by one of their staff as though it were a facsimile, without enquiring as to whether there was an original in existence, which there was. This understandably caused a certain amount of family irritation, in that the writing was nothing like that of the soldier in question, lacking its forthrightness and obvious individuality, but the fact remained that this was a statement about war and warfare of considerable distinction, marking out its author as a person of exceptional literacy, sensitivity and style.

The soldier in question was, of course, Roland Mountfort, whose remarkable, wartime letters form the basis of this present book; you will find the description quoted on page 94. His writings came to my notice as a result of an appeal I made in the *Radio Times* early in 1976, which asked for material to be sent to the BBC to assist in the making of a television documentary I was preparing to commemorate the sixtieth anniversary of the Battle of the Somme. In all, the corporation received 459 replies, resulting in a hugely impressive, indeed a heart-warming harvest, such was the enthusiasm of those who responded. Reply number 14 was from a Mr Neville Mountfort of Solihull, West Midlands, offering a number of letters written in 1916 by his half-brother Roland, formerly a member of the London-raised battalion, the 10th Royal Fusiliers, which went into action on 7 July 1916 as part of the second phase of the three-and-a-half-month campaign on the Somme.

My hope in making the appeal was that I would find a number of powerful first-hand quotations by soldiers who had fought on the Somme to be read by actors in the course of the programme. This was easily achieved, and the documentary was duly transmitted, under the title *The Battle of the Somme*, on 29 June 1976 on BBC-1. It can be fairly stated that the programme was a success, attracting a large and appreciative audience and being nominated both for a BAFTA in the UK and an International Emmy in the United States.

The programme concentrated almost exclusively on the battle's historic, disastrous first day, 1 July 1916; thus there was no place in it for Roland Mountfort since, as already indicated, his involvement in the campaign came later. This was, however, no cause for concern, because once the programme was transmitted, my next task would be to write the book which Messrs Dent had commissioned in the light of the sheer quality and range of the evidence that had been submitted in the wake of the *Radio Times* appeal. They had seen that appeal and contacted me to ask if there was any likelihood of a book in the material that was being sent to the BBC in response. I invited two of their directors to come and see, and when they surveyed the mass of letters, diaries, documents, drawings, postcards, photographs and ephemera of all kinds that had been despatched to me, in envelopes, parcels and packages of every description – not just relating to the Somme campaign but to many other aspects of the Western Front war – they had been greatly impressed by what they saw and had offered a contract there and then. I had no hesitation in accepting, in that it was clear that the appeal had revealed a substantial number of chroniclers whose writings, none of them previously published, were beyond question of very high calibre. Roland Mountfort was in the forefront of that list, and in the text which eventually went to the printers a year or so later he was a prominent contributor.

What was it that guaranteed him this role? His capacity for description has already been discussed, but also he had an unswerving honesty and a grip on reality that prevented him from disguising his emotions or mincing his words. Thus after a spell in trenches in appalling weather in February 1916 he stated: 'I don't like writing other than cheerful letters, but if I could compose one now I should be one of the most deserving VC heroes of the war.' Describing the start of the attack on the Somme on 7 July 1916 in which he was wounded, he reported: 'There was a good deal of shouting... but only necessary orders. We didn't dribble footballs, neither did we say "This way to Berlin, boys" nor any of the phrases employed weekly by the News of the World.' Arriving in London's Waterloo station to be driven off to hospital with his fellow casualties, he was less than impressed by the scenes with which he was confronted: 'There was the fat-headed crowd, just as you read about it, gaping and throwing cigarettes etc, and the whole ride was most detestable... with me perched up in front... with two days dirt and beard, hatless and dishevelled, and a dangling sleeve.' These statements might have come from an intelligent officer, but there is an extra value in Mountfort's evidence in that, although educated at Coventry's grammar school, where he had been a head of a sixth form, he had abjured all thought of a commission and had deliberately remained with the 'other ranks', the Poor Bloody Infantry of the Western Front war, accepting only the modest of elevation of becoming a Lance Corporal. Thus, for example, he was swift to condemn what he saw as the heavy burdens unnecessarily heaped on himself and his comrades as, newly arrived in France, they began their march from the Channel ports to the front in the summer of 1915. On 10 August he wrote: 'We walked fifteen miles on Wednesday. It doesn't sound much, but when you think of the heat of the day, the weight of the packs and the state of the French roads you will understand it was an amazing strain on our endurance. . . Our packs I cannot find word to describe. It is a cruel, unnatural weight that no man should be called upon to carry.' Add to all this the – in my view – supreme virtue that his judgements and attitudes, being conveyed in contemporary letters, necessarily catch the flavour of the moment; there is no hindsight here, no polishing of memories in retrospect. Roland Mountfort was a serious observer of a serious war chronicling his experiences as and when they happened, and therein lies his special value for the student of that now ninety-year-old conflict. His is an important voice well worth hearing.

While I was compiling *Tommy Goes to War* (which includes all the extracts just quoted), a further development occurred which ensured that researchers and historians other than myself would be able to take advantage of the emergence of Roland Mountfort as a notable witness of the First World War. As a result of a friendly initiative endorsed both by the BBC and the Imperial War Museum, some of the best of the material I had received following my appeal was transferred, with the full permission of the copyright holders, to the Museum's Department of Documents. Altogether over a hundred collections were accepted for permanent retention in the Museum's archives, many of them of considerable distinction, a fact which still gives me much satisfaction. Indeed, a number of them were deemed to be of such value that they are now conserved in handsomely bound volumes with their pages specially treated to pre-empt deterioration. One of those collections, it is hardly necessary for me to add in the present context, is the wartime correspondence of Roland Mountfort.

Some years later, in fact in 1989, I, as it were, followed in the footsteps of Roland Mountfort by becoming a freelance historian at the Imperial War Museum, being attached particularly to the Department of Documents, with the express mission of writing further books on the First World War with the museum's archives as the prime source. The third of these, of five, was published in 1996 under the title *The Imperial War Museum Book of the Somme.* Inevitably, while researching it, I turned to what was by this time the Roland Mountfort collection, including in my text two powerful and memorable quotations, together with a brief summary of his subsequent career, in a chapter on the battle's second, grimly attritional phase.

Roland Mountfort is therefore not merely a soldier whose writings I have long admired but one to whom I feel personally grateful for having helped me, albeit unknowingly, in the making of two of my favourite books. In view of all this, it gives me very great pleasure to see his letters made available to interested readers in this admirably edited and scholarly edition. For my part, I am honoured and delighted to have been given the opportunity to contribute this brief Preface. I would also like to congratulate all those involved in this enterprise and wish the book every success.

Malcolm Brown
July 2008

INTRODUCTION

Roland Mountfort was a Great War soldier who served on the Western Front, in 1915-1916, and in Africa, in 1917-1918. He had enlisted in the Royal Fusiliers in August 1914 and served with its 10th Battalion until he was wounded in July 1916 during the Battle of the Somme. On his recovery, he was drafted into the Regiment's 25th Battalion in Africa. By modern standards, Roland was a prolific letter writer who maintained a lengthy correspondence with his family throughout the war. Of those letters, 77 have survived and they describe his experiences in the Army between May 1915 and January 1918. The letters are now in the keeping of the Imperial War Museum; the circumstances in which they were donated to the Museum in 1976 have been explained by Malcolm Brown in his Preface.

It was Malcolm's use of Roland's letters in "Tommy Goes To War" and "The Imperial War Museum Book of the Somme"[1] that first alerted us to their existence. At the time, we were involved in a study of the part played in the Great War by former pupils of Roland's school in Coventry, our conclusions being published in 2005 in "Doing Its Part Nobly: Coventry's King Henry VIII School and the Great War". We wrote about Roland in that book but a chapter did scant justice to such a valuable collection of letters. We also produced a transcript of the letters for the School but soon felt that they deserved a wider readership. Although the decision to publish the letters was therefore an easy one to make, it was only possible with the support of the present day members of the Mountfort family, who not only gave us permission to reproduce the letters but have been unstinting in their assistance of our venture. (A full Acknowledgements section can be found on page 13).

Long before the letters came to our attention, their value had, of course, been appreciated by the Imperial War Museum, and we are grateful to Roderick Suddaby, The Keeper of the Department of Documents at the IWM, for endorsing our efforts:

"Ever since they were generously donated to the Imperial War Museum by his family in 1976, Roland Mountfort's First World War letters have been recognised by staff and historians alike as an outstanding personal record of the realities of trench warfare. We are therefore delighted that, through this book, all his surviving correspondence from the Western Front, and his few later letters home from East Africa, will now become available to a wider audience." (Letter, December 30th, 2005)

Roland Mountfort was born in Coventry in 1890 and educated at the city's grammar school. He subsequently worked in London with the Prudential Insurance Company and volunteered at the beginning of the war, along with many other employees of the Prudential. Although he was not a natural soldier, being too fastidious and too sceptical to relish life in the Army, he seems to have

---

[1] "Tommy Goes to War" is now published in a revised paperback edition by Tempus Publications; "The Imperial War Museum Book of the Somme" is published by Pan Macmillan .

been a good one. He was quickly made up to Lance Corporal and one senses that he fulfilled his duties conscientiously. He voluntarily gave up his 'stripe' when he joined the 25th Battalion of the Royal Fusiliers in South Africa, having no experience of that theatre of operations, but was soon prevailed upon to take it back. He felt a strong bond with his comrades: on hearing that his company had been on the receiving end of a heavy German bombardment whilst he was in the safety of a training school, he felt that "in a way I must congratulate myself on being here" but that, at the same time, "I feel that I should like to be with my pals if they have got to go through it". However, Roland also disliked many of the discomforts and much of the pettiness of Army life – "the piffling little trifles that constitute three fourths of the evils of army life". His was certainly not the classic case of 'disillusionment' – he appears to have entered the Army with few illusions in the first place. However, his commitment to the struggle survived the long years of hardship and even the loss of close friends. In an undemonstrative way, Roland was a patriot, albeit one with a small 'p'.

Roland's intellectual qualities, educational background and his obvious competence as a soldier must have made him potential officer material, even in the 10th Royal Fusiliers – the 'Stockbrokers' Battalion'. However, he chose to remain in the ranks and he served most of the war as a Lance Corporal. He finally applied for a commission in 1918 but this did not come through until 1919, shortly before his return to civilian life. Thus, this literate, shrewd and often witty observer looks at the war and at life in the Army from the perspective of the ranks. He may not be unique in that respect but he has nonetheless left us a valuable and stimulating collection of letters recounting a young man's experiences in the Army of 1914-18.

We have decided to reproduce Roland's letters in their entirety. He wrote with clarity and interest about all the facets of his life and his comments on family matters, literature and his spells away from the front are in themselves of interest and present a much fuller picture of the man and his time. They also produce a more balanced account of his experiences in the Great War and allow the writer's priorities to remain clear. As Malcolm Brown points out in his Preface: "there is no hindsight here, no polishing of memories in retrospect." His fellow historian Richard Holmes strikes a similar note in "Tommy": "Much better to get back to what people thought at the time ... the closer we get to events the better our chance of finding out how people really felt"[1]. Roland's letters give us such an opportunity, their spontaneity and freshness remarkably undiminished by the passage of time.

Chris Holland and Rob Phillips,

Coventry, July 2008

---

[1] *Richard Holmes: "Tommy: The British Soldier On The Western Front 1914 – 1918", Harper Perennial, 2005.*

ACKNOWLEDGEMENTS

First, and most obviously, we would like to thank the present day Mountfort family who have been unstinting in their support of this venture. Sue Martin, the copyright holder, kindly gave us permission to reproduce the letters and Bob Mountfort, Peter Mountfort and Maureen Selwood have provided a great deal of information about Roland and his family, as well as relevant photographs. Bob Mountfort kindly checked our final draft.

Malcolm Brown, who first alerted us to the existence of Roland's letters, has provided us with an excellent Preface and has always offered encouragement and support. We have been fortunate in being able to benefit from the experience of such a distinguished historian of the Great War. We have also benefited from the advice and help of Roderick Suddaby, Keeper of the Department of Documents at the Imperial War Museum, and we would also like to thank David Bell for kindly giving us permission to reproduce photographs from the Imperial War Museum's Photograph Archive. Ronnie Wilkinson of Pen and Sword Books Ltd kindly allowed us to reproduce the photograph of Foncquevillers churchyard on Page 83.

Clare Bunkham, formerly Assistant Archivist at the Prudential Insurance Company, provided us with useful information on the time that Roland and his close friends spent at the Prudential. The resources of the National Archives have been invaluable in helping provide the background for the letters. Sheila Woolf, formerly Head of English at King Henry VIII School, Coventry, kindly wrote the appendix assessing Roland's literary interests and Peter Huxford, Head of History at the same school, has proof-read the text. We would like to acknowledge the financial support provided by the School's Parents' Association for the original transcription of the letters in 2004. The School's Headmaster, George Fisher, has always been a keen supporter of the venture. Others who have given us help are Chris Baker, Diane Holland and John Haviland. Finally, we would like to thank Professor Richard Holmes for permission to quote from his book "Tommy: The British Soldier on the Western front 1914-1918".

~

THE TEXT

We have made almost no changes to the original text. The occasional spelling mistake and the equally rare duplication of words have been corrected and a small number of minor alterations to punctuation have been made, usually the addition of commas, to facilitate the reading of the text. One or two very long paragraphs have been split. The more we have worked on the letters, the more we have been struck by the quality of Roland's English, especially when you consider the difficult circumstances in which many of his letters were written. We have repositioned some of the text from its order in the IWM collection. The main changes made are in Chapter 2, where all the letters are undated. Reasons are given in each case. Footnotes have been added where appropriate.

The context of the letters is explained and some dates and names have been included where this helps clarification. These additions have been placed in square brackets. Finally, a brief summary of contents precedes each letter to help those who may be looking for specific subject matter.

Main Abbreviations Used In The Letters

ack^d	*acknowledged*	*LCC*	*London County Council*
app^d	*appointed*	*L/Cpl*	*Lance Corporal*
A.S.C.	*Army Service Corps*	*NCO*	*Non Commissioned Officer*
Ass^t	*Assistant*	*No.*	*number*
Batt^n	*Battalion*	*p.c.*	*post card*
Captn	*Captain*	*Pln*	*Platoon*
C.B.	*Confined to Barracks*	*P.O.*	*Post Office*
chq	*cheque*	*pol*	*policy*
C.O.	*Commanding Officer*	*pr*	*pair*
comm^n	*commission*	*Prudtl*	*Prudential*
compt	*compartment*	*QMS*	*Quartermaster Sergeant*
Coy	*Company*	*R.B.*	*Rifle Brigade*
CQMS	*Company Quartermaster*	*rec^d*	*received*
	Sergeant	*reg^d*	*registered*
dept	*department*	*reg^{ns}*	*regulations*
Div^l	*Divisional*	*R.F.*	*Royal Fusiliers*
Div^n	*Division*	*R.F.A.*	*Royal Field Artillery*
D^r	*Doctor*	*R.G.A.*	*Royal Garrison Artillery*
encs	*enclosure*	*Sgt*	*Sergeant*
Expd	*Expeditionary*	*Sgt Mjr*	*Sergeant Major*
Genl	*General*	*sol^r / sol^s*	*solicitor / solicitors*
G.O.C.	*General Officer Commanding*	*Sub*	*Sub Lieutenant*
insce	*insurance*	*W.O.*	*War Office*
KRR	*The King's Royal Rifle Corps*		

Chapter 1

BACKGROUND

Roland Mountfort was born in Coventry on March 7th, 1890, the fourth son of Joseph Mountfort. Joseph's father, also called Joseph, had moved to Coventry from Leicestershire and had entered banking in 1830. He went on to become manager of the local branch of the Coventry and Warwickshire Banking Company, which amalgamated with Lloyds Bank in 1879. Joseph senior's three sons followed their father into the same bank.

Joseph junior also went on to become a bank manager. He married three times and fathered eleven children. Roland's mother, Joseph's second wife, was Hannah Margaret Dormor. She died when Roland was three years old and his father remarried. Roland was therefore brought up from an early age by his step-mother, Sarah, and most of his wartime letters are addressed to her. Sarah was only 23 at the time of her marriage, 21 years younger than her husband, and she took on responsibility for Joseph's four sons. In addition, she bore Joseph a further seven children between 1896 and 1906.

The siblings mentioned most frequently in Roland's correspondence are his half-brother Vincent ('Vin'), who was eleven years his senior; his natural brother Dormor, who was two years older; his half-sister Gwyneth, seven years his junior; and his half-brother Geoffrey, who was nine years younger. Both Dormor and Geoffrey were also to serve in the First World War, Dormor with the Surrey Yeomanry and Geoffrey, like Roland, with the Royal Fusiliers. (A full family tree can be found in Appendix 1).

The Mountforts had strong interests in the arts. The men of the family, in particular, all aspired to writing, composing and art, taking their lead from Roland's father. A modern-day member of the family describes them as "the last of the Victorian gentlemen" – intellectuals rather than practical men, although the eldest son, Louis, went on to become an engineer of some distinction. These family interests were imbibed by Roland and are constantly reflected in his letters. (An analysis of his literary tastes can be found in Appendix 2).

Although the need for his sons to make a living would have been a clear imperative from Joseph Mountfort, Roland was nonetheless raised in comfortable circumstances. The 1901 census shows that the family had a general domestic servant and a nurse living on the premises; the family homes, first in Grosvenor Road, then in Manor Road and finally in Park Road, were solid middle class houses in a salubrious area on the southern side of Coventry, within 15 minutes walking distance of the city centre. Despite the premature death of his mother, the Mountfort household would have provided a secure and lively environment for the young Roland, with the bustle of a large family and the stimulus of companions with a strong interest in the arts. The intellectual self-confidence that was to mark Roland's wartime letters was an obvious consequence of this background.

Joseph Mountfort had attended King Henry VIII School for a short time in the 1860s and he sent six sons to be educated there. Roland entered the School in 1898, at the age of eight, and left in 1905. At the time, the School was still commonly known in Coventry as 'The Grammar School' – the title 'King Henry VIII School' had only come into regular use in the 1880s when the School moved to its present site on Warwick Road. Although there were still a number of boarders, most of its pupils were day boys drawn from the local professions and trades – the introduction of scholarship places, which achieved some social widening of the School's intake, did not take place until 1907. Most day pupils lived close to the School – Roland would only have had a few minutes walk to the School gates.

In Roland's day the School was of modest size and struggling both financially and academically. An inspection in 1905, the year Roland left, was critical of several matters connected with the teaching and discipline, and the School roll had fallen below one hundred. Thereafter, the School's fortunes gradually revived. Despite its problems, the School did not lack an esprit de corps and, for its size, supported a surprisingly large number of teams and societies.

Roland makes no mention of his school days in his letters. However, he was a successful pupil and one assumes that he enjoyed his time at King Henry's. He was young by comparison with his classmates but he did well academically and went on to win a Simon Stone scholarship. He also played a full part in the School's life, appearing in plays and concerts and belonging to debating societies. He was not a noted sportsman but did win his 2nd XI Cricket colours. During his last year he was Head of Form VIb and was placed first in the form, distinguishing himself in Science and French.

In a later age Roland would doubtless have gone on to university and he would have been well-suited to study at that level. However, comparatively few of the School's pupils at that time progressed to higher education. Instead, in 1905, Roland entered and passed the Civil Service Copyists' Exam – as his brother Dormor had done the year before. One senses a father's hand directing his sons towards a 'useful' vocational qualification. Roland left School at the end of the academic year in 1905, at the age of 15.

Just over a year later, on August 13th, 1906, Roland joined the Postal Department of the London-based Prudential Insurance Company, transferring to the Solicitors' Department in 1909. He was to work at the firm's Holborn Offices in the years leading up to the outbreak of war and again once the war had finished. It was at the Prudential that he formed some of his closest friendships, notably with Bill Morris and Claude Fryer. The 1911 census shows that Roland was living in lodgings in Leytonstone on the north-eastern outskirts of London and about seven miles from Holborn. A fellow lodger was Ernest Pickering, who became another close friend and enlisted in the same battalion as Roland in 1914. He is described as a clerk in a mineral water company. Roland's brother, Dormor, was living at the same address; he was also employed as an insurance clerk, although with the Royal Insurance Company.

~

Chapter 2

ENGLAND, MAY – JULY 1915
LETTERS 1-7

Roland enlisted soon after the outbreak of hostilities in August 1914. He was to be one of more than 9,000 Prudential men who served in the war. The company was strongly supportive of the war effort, making up the difference between service pay and normal salaries and guaranteeing jobs to those who returned from war service that would be "no less advantageous" than those that had been given up. By October 1915, 70% of eligible clerical staff had volunteered, with the rest being urged to follow. Nearly 800 Prudential men died in the war – 8.6% of those who had served.

Roland's surviving letters date from May 1915, so we know next to nothing about his early experiences in the Army. What we do know is that he joined the 10th Battalion of the Royal Fusiliers, the so-called "Stockbrokers' Battalion". It was a K2 battalion – part of the second hundred thousand to respond to Kitchener's appeal for volunteers – and was made up of employees from the City. Raised by Major the Hon. Robert White, at the suggestion of Sir Henry Rawlinson, Director of Recruiting, it is arguably the first of the famous pals battalions. A recruiting office was opened on August 21st, 1914, and by August 27th 1,600 had been enrolled; presumably Roland was one. On the 29th the Battalion was inspected by Lord Roberts in Temple Gardens, with the men parading "in all sorts of clothing, from silk hats and morning coats to caps and Norfolk jackets".[1] The men were sworn in and a few days later, on September 3rd, the Battalion proceeded to Colchester and began training. Initially living in tents, the Fusiliers moved into barrack accommodation in October.

In late February 1915, the Battalion joined the 111th Brigade, 37th Division on Salisbury Plain for its final training before going overseas. At first, the soldiers were billeted in Andover but moved to camp at Windmill Hill on April 7th, where they stayed until embarkation at the end of July. Training included physical drill and route marches, practice on the rifle ranges, night manoeuvres, sham attacks and defensive actions; field days developed unit co-ordination, first within the Battalion, later at Brigade and Divisional levels.

The letters commence during Roland's time on Salisbury Plain. The early letters are undated but would appear to begin in May 1915.

~

---

[1] *'The Royal Fusiliers in the Great War' by H. C. O'Neill.*

[No. 1 – domestic matters – post card of company – delay in going to the front]

A tea shop
Andover
Wed.
[probably May 5th]

Dear Mother,

Your letter just rec^d, I am sorry I forgot to drop a line on my arrival here. I didn't get an opportunity to do it immediately, as I generally do, & afterwards it slipped my memory. When I did write, although I addressed the letter to Gwyneth, of course I meant it to be to all of you; but I thought it was Gwyneth's turn to receive it. You may be quite sure if I were offended at anything I should speak up about it.

I am at Andover en route for Oxford; & having some time to wait, am having tea. I was due to go last Monday, but at the last moment was told to go to-day. I return on Sunday night. My ankle is still rather swollen & uncomfortable; but I have managed to get my boot on & get along pretty well.

I enclose for you a p.c. of C Company marching thro' Andover. We wore white hat bands as we were the enemy that day. You see me enjoying the uncoveted honour of Commanding Officer's orderly, on his left. He (Col. White)[1] is the old boy with white bands round his arms. The other, our ex-Adjutant Capt. Egerton Warburton, is now at the front.[2]

The Battⁿ you refer to is not ours. Also the delay in going to the front is not peculiar to our Battⁿ, but to the whole of Kitchener's Army. The First Army[3] is in process of going now;[4] & we, the Second, will go in due course.

I also enclose for you to keep for me a photo of Pickering[5]. He has had to grow his moustache again, so looks rather different actually.

Best love to all, R.

~

---

[1] *Colonel White*: formerly, Major the Hon R. White, whose efforts had resulted in the raising of the 10th Battalion of the Royal Fusiliers – see background section to this chapter. White had taken command of the Battalion in November 1914.

[2] *Warburton is now at the front*: Egerton Warburton left the Battalion on March 31st; the march through Andover probably refers to one of the field days earlier that same month.

[3] *First Army*: the first six divisions of Kitchener's New Armies – the so-called K1 divisions. These were drawn from the first volunteers who had responded to the Secretary of State's appeal for volunteers in August 1914. So great was the response that another five New Armies were created. These groupings did not, however, correspond with the numbering of operational field armies.

[4] *The First Army is in the process of going out now*: the 9th Division had crossed to France by May 12th.

[5] *Pickering*: Ernest Pickering, a close pre-war friend of Roland. See Page 16.

[No. 2 – *training* – *church parade* – *a weekend pass* – *Morris* – *rifle butts* – *a near mutiny*]

No. 9 Platoon 10 RF
Windmill Hill Camp
Ludgershall
Andover
Saturday
[May 15th]

Dear Mother,

Will you please thank Gwyneth and Sheila for their letters. I must write in rather a hurry, or you won't get this to-morrow (perhaps you won't as it is) & I should like you to do that in case you are thinking of writing to me. We are going on a 5 days march, starting early Monday morning & returning Friday. We are sleeping in barns &c except Thursday night, when we are bivouacing. It won't be much use writing till the end of the week, as I imagine we shan't get them delivered.

I spent last week end with Morris. I had an awful job to get my pass. No. 9 Platoon was for duty on Friday & I took it for granted I should be on fatigue. When I discovered I had escaped that, I put in my pass, only to be informed later that I couldn't go, as they hadn't got a sufficient number for Church Parade, if you please, on Sunday morning. Church Parade here lasts about half an hour. Five Batt[ns] participate forming 3 sides of a square & the chaplain takes post in the centre. No one can hear a word except those in the front rank, & the ranks in rear have therefore to amuse themselves as best they can, & their amusement, since there is no one to watch them, usually takes the form of playing pitch & toss,[1] grousing about the army, & a variety of similar things not usually associated with a divine service. For an institution of this description they had every intention of stopping, in our platoon alone, six men's week end leave. And what, do you imagine, is the explanation of their keenness? The welfare of the souls of men who are going to endanger their bodies, of course you reply. Wrong. The chaplain is paid according to the number of men he preaches to.

The business appeared to us so iniquitous that we resolved to exert all our energies to get our leave by hook or by crook. Without boring you with details of the process, I may say that I spent Saturday morning in half hours of alternate hope that I should succeed & conviction that I should not until it was too late to catch the train, when I sent a wire cancelling my visit, & therefore immediately received my pass signed. We rushed off to the station at once, but the train had gone. We noticed however that the signals were against it, & it had stopped some 300 yards down the line, & after a brief consultation we performed some masterly scouting manoeuvres down the line, taking cover behind telegraph poles, &

---

[1] *pitch and toss*: a game of chance in which coins are thrown at a determined point, such as a stick, with the player landing his coin nearest to the point being the winner; he then has the chance to toss all the coins, winning those that land heads up. See Kipling's poem "If":
> If you can make one heap of all your winnings
> And risk it on one turn of pitch and toss.

notices warning trespassers they would be prosecuted, until we reached the train; when, creeping gingerly along close beneath it to escape the vigilance of the guard, we climbed up from the track into the nearest 3rd compt. rather I think to the indignation of its occupants, but much to our own relief that we were safe to spend the next thirty hours in London, instead of in the guard room.

I spent a quiet time at Morris's. The only thing we did of note was to go to Southend on the bike[1] on Sunday morning. Subsequently a Zeppelin paid us the sincerest form of flattery & visited the same place.[2] I am sorry we missed it.

I arrived back here about 2 a.m. on Monday morning, & one of the persons I trod on on our entering the tent took a dastardly revenge by rousing up to tell me that breakfast was at 6.15 a.m., parade at 7, to mark at the Butts at Bulford, 7 miles away, for the K.R.R. It was even as he said, & I spent a long & tiring day, until 6 p.m. marking at the rottenest butts[3] I ever saw. They were recently constructed by the Canadians, & consist merely of a trench & a mound. Bullets go humming away over the back at every volley; while the markers have no overhead cover at all, & every time a bullet ricochets (i.e. strikes the earth before the target) you are showered with stones & chalk. Standing in the sun all day gave me a headache; & after tea I was beginning to revive when the orders came out for the next day. Markers, reveille 3.30 a.m., parade 4.15. We got back about 1.30 that day. The next day we shot ourselves (I don't mean suicide) – parade 7.15 a.m., returned 8.30 p.m. Next morning, ditto, reveille 3.30 a.m., parade 4.15 a.m. And then we had a rather interesting time.

The Sgt. Major was due to wake the Coy, as that hour they don't blow reveille. The night before, he got beastly drunk; & when the sentry woke him promptly went to sleep again. At 4 o'clock he was again aroused by the Cook Sgt. who had got our breakfast ready. This time he got up & called up the Coy. Parade was at 4.15, which gave us exactly a quarter of an hour to dress, have breakfast, see to our rifles & get on parade. The result was of course that before we were dressed they served out breakfast; & before we could touch that they were yelling out "Come on parade". It was raining in torrents, & no one was in the best of tempers. Some stopped to snatch a mouthful of bread & butter, some didn't have time to do that, but anyway, at 4.15 the only men out were the 4 officers & the Sgt Mjr & the whole Coy was reported as being late on parade. The same thing happened in D Coy. We got away about 4.30. It rained hard all day – a heavy & bitterly cold rain – I daresay you had it – last Thursday. There was no shelter, & by 6 we were drenched. We finished firing at 2.30, having been out 10 hours. The only relief in the monotony was a visit from the Colonel & our Company Commander – the Major's successor – when the latter made a little speech about things. He said the Company had disgraced itself; he was once proud to command us, now he wasn't; & he was considering what steps would be taken as to

---

[1] *the bike*: see photograph on Page 81.
[2] *Subsequently a Zeppelin ... visited the same place*: Southend was attacked by Zeppelin LZ 38 on the night of Sunday, May 9th / Monday, May 10th.
[3] *marking at the butts*: recording the accuracy of those shooting at the rifle range, with the markers usually positioned in a trench beneath the targets and reporting the scores either by flags and/or by returning the targets by means of a pulley system. The Battalion was shooting at the Butts on Monday, May 10th.

punishment. As we considered an injury had been done to us in bringing us out at all, his speech didn't make him very popular. Four other Batt[ns] were due to shoot that day, & we were the only one that turned out. Fourteen men who went to a portable coffee stall without permission had their names taken & were subsequently given 3 days C.B. Our Company Commander referred to us once during the day as "this rotten Company". By the end of the day, when we got back to our tents with everything soaked through & the water squelching in our boots we were pretty fed up. The next morning 26 men of C Coy & 36 of D went sick. At the sick parade everybody cheered them. When the C.O. heard of it he went round & had out the Medical Officer; & told him he considered most of the men were perfectly fit, & he was to show no leniency. I don't quite understand exactly what happened; but at any rate the C.O. spoke to the D[r]. in such a way before the men that the D[r]. promptly resigned & went off the same night. By the afternoon the spirit in both C & D Coy's was perfectly mutinous. The 14 men who got C.B. insisted on being taken up to the C.O. to protest. The Sgt Mjr tried to excuse himself by throwing the blame at the orderly Sgt, who immediately started to tell him what he thought about him. The knot of spectators took the part of the orderly Sgt so vigorously that one was marched off to the guard-room. The orderly Sgt's reputation being at stake, he insisted on being taken up to the C.O. The NCO's of the Company consulted together & decided to make the Company Commander apologise for the way he addressed us, or they would resign in a body. All afternoon knots of men stood about in the camp in the way men will when things are fermenting & I'm sure it only wanted one spark of insult from anyone in authority to set the whole situation ablaze. But the C.O., with greater wisdom than he knew, promised to go into the case on Monday, & the Company Commander when the NCO's sought him had rushed off on leave with a note to his second in command (a very decent sort) to "handle the situation", & the Sgt Mjr got into a dickens of a funk & appealed to the NCO's "for God's sake to keep the men under control" & no one can quarrel with a man in a funk; so everything is standing over; & to stand over, in a case of this description, is to simmer down & generally settle, so I doubt if there will be any great excitement on Monday – especially as we shall be out of camp for 5 days. In any other Batt[n] the men would never have put up with the mismanagement & annoyances we have done. The Gordon Highlanders at Tidworth[1] refused to come on parade once when they had had no breakfast. They said "No breakfast, no parade" & the powers were helpless. Similar things have happened in the Gloucesters & other regiments. But we, being clerks & not miners or dockers, have no idea of union or concerted action, & the powers of it, & have no remedy for our ills. But C Coy since we lost our old Major & Sgt Major & got a couple of rotters in their places have put up with so much that I think even they will turn at last; & I rather think our blundering old fool of a Colonel[2] is beginning to see it. I forgot to say that at first, as their punishment for being late on parade the leave of the whole Company was stopped, but afterwards that was rescinded, as the C.O. said the offence was "too

---

[1] *Tidworth*: a garrison town on the edge of Salisbury Plain.
[2] *Our blundering old fool of a Colonel*: in his diary, Colonel Robert White confined his comments on the incident to: "May 13th: Companies turned out late on parade. Spoke to N.C.O.'s."

serious & disquieting for punishment". I quite believe he found it "disquieting" enough.

If I don't have a chance to let you know where we are during the week, I will write afterwards & let you know all about it.

With best love to all,

Yours affectly

Roland

∼

[No. 3 – a Zeppelin raid – Brigade training exercise – rumours – an unwelcome promotion – fine weather]

PS. The Zeppelins dropped bombs on Leytonstone[1] & killed one person I think. Morris[2] heard them distinctly, but the bombs fell some way away from his show.

No. 9 Platoon 10 RF

&c

Tuesday

[probably June 8th]

Dear Mother,

Just a short note, as there's nothing on earth to write about.

I have been expecting to hear from either you or Gwyneth during the week end. I hope you are all well. Auntie Annie says she has not heard from Dormor for quite a long while, & wants to know if you have heard anything of him. Would you mind telling me when you heard last, & what he was doing.

We went out – the whole brigade – for another 2 days last week.[3] We bivouacked in a very stony field, but it didn't worry me much for I was on outpost until 2, & after that I could have slept on anything. The next day we fought a rear-guard action – the 10th against the rest of the brigade. The country we crossed was all hills like the side of a house, & the day (Thurs) was <u>blazing</u>. I never felt so exhausted in all my life. Think of the clothes we wear & the weight we carry, & of running up hill with the Thermometer at 80 or over in the shade. When you get a halt you collapse, more than lie down, like a sack of sawdust, & put your face on the cool grass. It's rather a fine sensation.

There are rumours about again about the front in 3 weeks &c, but there's nothing to show there's anything in them. They have served us out with active service boots, to be worn for a few days & then handed in to be kept against our going out. It only signifies that they seem to think we may go some day.

---

[1] *The Zeppelins dropped bombs on Leytonstone*: probably a reference to a raid on Leytonstone that took place on the night of Monday, May 31st / Tuesday, June 1st.
[2] *Leytonstone & Morris*: Leytonstone was the London suburb where Roland had lived before the war, which was also the home of Bill Morris, a close friend and colleague of Roland at the Prudential.
[3] *We went out ... for another 2 days last week*: a two-day exercise was held on June 3rd-4th – suggesting the date of the letter is June 8th.

I hear from Morris that one of the juniors in the Sol^s Dep^t – an absolutely hopeless idiot, whom I have anathematised to his face times without number when endeavouring to knock information into his stupid head – a stupid, conceited, effeminate boy of 21 – is obtaining a commission in this Batt^n. I don't believe it yet, but if it's true I'm looking forward to seeing him.

The weather has been consistently fine & hot for some time now. I sleep outside the tent nearly every night. The early mornings are pretty fresh & sometimes my top blanket is sopping with dew. I nearly always wake up just after sunrise – going to sleep again, of course. As I lie, without moving my head I can see woods and hills for 5 miles or more, & the dawn is often very beautiful. But after living amongst them for so long & getting so fed up I'm afraid the beauties of nature don't appeal to us much.

I shall be pleased to hear when you have time to write. I believe we are marching all night to-morrow night. I hear that Lily Jones is in St. Thomas's Hospital, having undergone an operation for something or other. I never hear from Waters Upton[1]. How are they going on? With best love to all,

Yours affectionately

Roland

~

[No. 4 – problems with dust – Royal inspection]

Camp
Friday
[June 25th]

Dear Mother,

Thanks for your letter enclosing Dormor's (which you are right in supposing I saw at Vin's) & also for your letter card received to-day. It depends upon what the contents of the letter from the Bank are, as to whether I want to see it or not. If it's merely a circular or something that doesn't want attention it doesn't matter about it, but if it's anything else you might send it down. I wrote to them the other day enquiring the amount of my balance & they replied. I don't think it can be about that.

I am sorry to hear of Gwyneth's disappointment. She will have to be content to go to Vin's[2]. I am sure he will have her – & be only too pleased to – if she likes to ask him to fix a date.

We have just had a very severe thunderstorm, the first rainfall for well over a month. The dust had become a very serious nuisance. We used to come back from marches in certain directions quite white from head to toe. In the main street of

---

[1] *Waters Upton*: the Shropshire hamlet that was the original home of Roland's step-mother, Sarah.
[2] *content to go to Vin's*: Vincent Mountfort, Roland's half-brother, lived in London. The nature of 'Gwyneth's disappointment' is not known but Gwyneth would have been about 19 at this time and the disappointment may relate to a job for which she had applied.

Ludgershall[1] it was quite ankle deep, & of course, by the time the first few men had passed, the rest of the column marches through a cloud. I have known the men 10 yards ahead to become quite invisible for short periods. In this chalky neighbourhood it has a peculiar fine & sticky nature, like a powder. On the face it settles thickly on the eyelids, eyebrows & moustache, giving the men a very funny appearance.

The whole Division was inspected by the King this morning.[2] He has been here since Wednesday, sleeping at nights in his train at Ludgershall station. We rehearsed the whole business yesterday. It must have been rather a fine sight for spectators, of whom there were not many, the inspection taking place about 3 miles away towards the middle of the plain. I suppose there were about 20,000 men on parade – artillery, cavalry, infantry, A.S.C. etc. etc. I was in the front rank and saw him very close to. He was on horseback & looked rather fit. Nevertheless his face is very wrinkled & worried looking. We had the same old rigmarole afterwards – the King had told our Colonel personally that he thought they were a fine lot of men & so forth, & that he would remember the Batt[n] individually as one of the best he had inspected. No doubt he told the other dozen or more the same thing.

I heard the King speak. You will be surprised to hear he did it just like an ordinary man.

I was due to go on leave this week end, but this Coy is finding Battalion duty, Brigade duty & Divisional duty, so it's at least 150 to 1 I don't get it. If I do I shall spend it with Morris & Fryer[3].

Give my regards to Frank Spencer[4] if you see him, they want recruits for the reserve of this Batt[n] if he wants to join an infantry reg[t].

I am sorry you couldn't read parts of my last letter. You didn't miss much. If there's anything important you failed to decipher, send it back & I'll elucidate. For my own part I can't see that it matters whether anything I find to write about in this hole is legible or not.

Best love to all. I hope you are all well. Thank Gwyneth for her letter. I shall be pleased to have Dormor's letter & will forward it to Vin.

Yours affectionately

Roland

~

---

[1] *Ludgershall*: the major railway centre for supplying the Army on Salisbury Plain.
[2] *The whole Division was inspected by the King this morning*: George V inspected the 37th Division on Silbury Hill on June 25th.
[3] *Fryer*: Claude Fryer, another close friend and colleague of Roland and Bill Morris. Claude Fryer joined the Solicitors' Department in 1907, to which Bill Morris transferred in 1908 and Roland in 1909. See photograph on Page 81.
[4] *Frank Spencer*: a family friend from Coventry. See photograph on Page 82.

[No. 5 – weekend leave – embarkation preparations – possible leave – other units departing]

Camp
Thursday **[July 8th]**

Dear Mother,

Thanks very much for your letter & please thank the children for theirs. I am glad they like the idea of going away. I don't know anything about either Aberystwith or Barmouth so can't advise you. I suppose you are determined to go to N. Wales. I should be inclined to try somewhere fresh – Torquay or Folkestone, or Hastings, or something of that sort. Still, no doubt Wales combines many advantages.

I got my postponed week end last week. Neither Morris nor Fryer being able to place much time at my disposal owing to the prior calls of wife & fiancée respectively (whom they will see every day for the rest of their lives) I went down to Oxford[1] on Saturday night. On Sunday morning we went a spin in the car around Wantage & Clifton Hampden.

I hope to have some news for you shortly. All leave is stopped after Sunday week & preparations are being made to leave here of such a nature as to leave no doubt we are going to the front. The Col. says the date of embarkation has been fixed & he knows it, but isn't at liberty to disclose it.

Meanwhile 30% of the Batt[n] are going to have 3 days leave in batches concluding on Sunday week. I don't suppose I shall get it; but if I do I shall have my teeth seen to in London & then come down to Coventry. Some fellows started this morning & were in a deuce of a fix, because the 15th Div[n]. has been going out for the last 3 days[2] from Tidworth & there are no trains running. They have been trying all sorts of ways – walking to Hungerford to the G.W.R., or walking to Andover & catching a train up to Swindon & going on from there.

The Gordon Highlanders left yesterday[3] afternoon. We were over in that direction attacking trenches, & during an armistice a crowd of our fellows went down & saw them off. I didn't go myself, but I hear that although a number of them were pretty well oiled & noisy, others seemed to feel the seriousness of it, & the scene on the whole was rather impressive.

You say in your letter "I wish you would ask us to send Dormor's letters back". Do you mean Vin? If so, I write very seldom, but will mention it when I do, if I remember.

I hope you enjoy yourself at Waters Upton. If I could have got this leave I might have come over with you for an hour or two, though there wouldn't be much time.

I hope you are all well. With best love from

Yours affectionately

Roland

---

[1] *I went down to Oxford*: Oxford was the birthplace of Roland's mother, Hannah, and Roland may still have had contacts with her family.
[2] *the 15th Division has been going out ...*: the 15th Division received orders to mobilise on July 4th and started crossing to France on July 8th, suggesting the letter was written on July 8th.
[3] *The Gordon Highlanders left yesterday*: the 9th (Service) and 10th (Service) Battalions of the Gordon Highlanders were part of the 15th Division.

[No. 6 – return from embarkation leave – divisional route march – embarkation preparations]

Camp, Monday
[July 19th]

Dear Mother,

I arrived here at about a quarter to 3 this morning.[1] The N.W. train was late at Euston, having to stop & change engines at Bletchley. Those engines are always going wrong. Having still plenty of time however, I walked up the Tottenham Ct. Rd. as far as Oxford St. to have a final glimpse of London before proceeding to Waterloo. I slept practically all the way down here, but in spite of that, & the 3 hours I had in bed here I was profusely disinclined to get up this morning. I think it's the grub that makes one so sleepy. For two days I had had enough to eat. On about half enough 3 hours sleep is quite sufficient for one night.

We went for a Div[l] route march to-day – about 15 miles. A Div[n] takes about 5 hours to pass a given spot.

I enclose (if I can get them in the envelope) some gloves of Gwyneth's. I warned her what would happen to them.

Preparations for going out are proceeding apace. They have served out tonight our active service pay-books, identification disks & field dressings. To-morrow we are giving in our spare uniform & boots. A rumour gives the actual date as the 27th.

With best love to all.

Yrs affectionately

Roland

P.S. Love to Hilda, & I hope she gets on all right with her exam.

∼

---

[1] *I arrived here at about a quarter to 3 this morning*: consistent with 'the 3 days leave in batches concluding on Sunday week' mentioned in the previous letter – suggesting the date of this letter is July 19th.

[No. 7 – domestic matters – battalion confined to camp]

Camp. Saturday
[July 24th]

Dear Mother,

Thanks very much for your letter & cutting. Aucuth is a very well known name in the Prudential. I don't know this son, but his father is a sub-manager & his uncle is one of the bosses of the Approved Society.

I am writing to wish you very many happy returns of to-morrow[1] & I enclose what you will have to look upon as my birthday present, as I am too isolated to get anything else. I hope you will all have a very happy holiday. If they send us up into the firing line soon enough I may spend it with you yet – in a bath chair.

Everyone is confined to camp after mid-night to-night.[2] Anyone absent then will be dealt with as absent on active service – so they say; but as the penalty is death I hardly think they will enforce it.

Everyone seems to think we *[ends]*

∼

---

[1] *many happy returns of tomorrow*: Sarah's birthday was July 25th, making the date of the letter July 24th.

[2] *Everyone is confined to camp after mid-night to-night*: presumably in preparation for the move overseas.

Chapter 3

FRANCE, AUGUST 1915 – JUNE 1916
LETTERS 8-37

Letters 8 – 37 cover Roland's period of service in France up until the Battle of the Somme in 1916, during which he was wounded.

At the end of July 1915, the 111th Brigade, 37th Division, of which the 10th Battalion, Royal Fusiliers was a part, was sent overseas. On July 30th, the Battalion was transported by train from Ludgershall to Folkestone, whence it made the short crossing to Boulogne, arriving in France just before midnight. The other battalions that made up the Brigade were the 13th Battalion of The King's Royal Rifle Corps, the 13th Battalion of the Rifle Brigade and the 13th Battalion of the Royal Fusiliers.

The emphasis in these letters is far more on the discomforts than the dangers of life in the line. The letters were obviously liable to censorship and Roland would have been concerned, in any case, not to worry his family more than necessary. They also, of course, reflect the personality of the writer. Roland's half brother, Neville, recalls that Roland was "a most fastidious man, particularly in regard to personal appearance and cleanliness", temperamentally unsuited to the rough and ready life of a soldier in wartime. Not surprisingly, Roland dwells on some of the privations of his time in the trenches.

However, the letters also mirror the experience of his Battalion during this period. After their introduction to life in the trenches, the 10th Royal Fusiliers were involved in line-holding. Although placed on stand-by during the Allied offensives of September 1915, the Battalion was not involved in a major engagement until the Battle of the Somme in 1916, though it was, of course, subjected to the constant attrition of trench warfare. The experiences of Guy Chapman, a junior officer in the 13th Royal Fusiliers, also part of the 111th Brigade, mirrored those of Roland and his comrades in the 10th Battalion. Of those 11 months, Chapman later stated that "warfare was a matter of learning the job" and he wrote of the "simplicity" of his Battalion on the eve of the Somme. "All we had learned had been to try and keep our trenches healthy, and to suffer shell and trench mortar fire ... Actually we knew very little."[1]

~

---

[1] Guy Chapman: "A Passionate Prodigality", 1933.

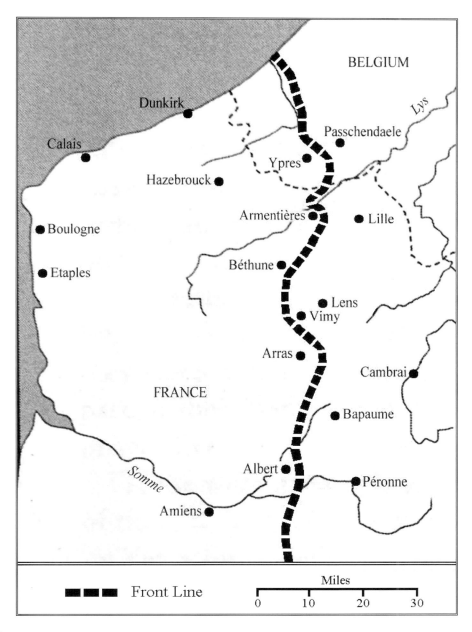

The Western Front, 1915

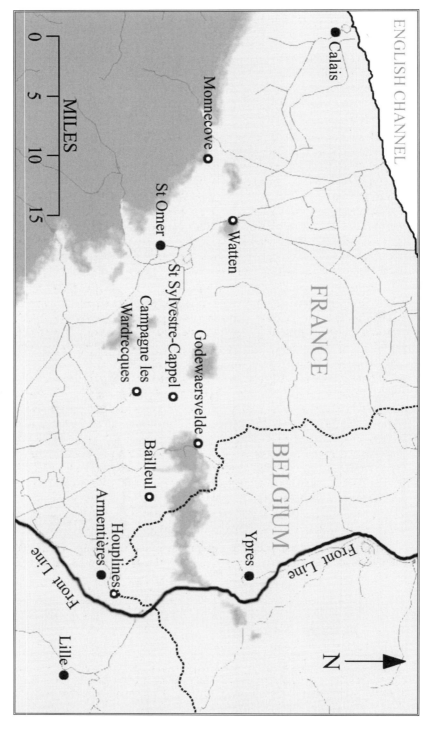

In the trenches: August 1915
(Letters 8-11)

[No. 8 – arrival in France – journey to Monnecove – first impressions of France]

PS. I imagine we are about
30 miles S.S.W. of where
we believe Dormor to be.

No Stk 771 L/Cpl RDM
Pln & Regt as before
British Expd Force
2nd August 1915

Dear Mother,

There's precious little to write about at present, but at the same time there's nothing to do, so I may as well tell you as much as I may of what has happened so far. We embarked at Folkestone & arrived in France about midnight *[at Boulogne]*.[1] We then marched a couple of miles to a camp, where we spent the rest of the night. The next morning after breakfast we marched another 3 miles to a railway station from which, after a long wait, we travelled in cattle trucks at 42 men to the truck, to the village where we now are *[Monnecove near Watten]*. The railway journey was longish, & not particularly interesting. There is nothing whatever to remind you that you are in France – the scenery is very similar to parts of England, & there are few indications of the war.

We are in a very ordinary village here, billeted in barns, & having as pleasant & a softer time than we used in our days of brigade training I have told you of. Except in the language of the inhabitants it is exactly like an English village. The children are pretty little beggars but pester you for souvenirs – sous[2] or cigarettes are what they ask in particular, & the smallest boys will smoke pipes or cigarettes with great enjoyment.

There are three public houses or "estaminets"[3] we are allowed to use – all much of a muchness, both as to appearance & stock in trade. The latter consists almost entirely of a fearful thin beer, sour as vinegar, vin rouge, vin blanc and cognac. The bar is in the front room, & is merely a small dock, like a county court witness box, in one corner with a few shelves behind. I have not encountered an inhabitant who speaks English yet, but almost all of us know enough French to carry on an entente cordiale. English money is taken at the rate of 10d[4] a franc; beer is 2 sous a glass & red wine 1 franc 75c a bottle. The latter is a sort of claret I believe, & not bad stuff.

We are resting now, but hope to get a move on soon. We are 17 miles from the firing line; & hear the heavy artillery from time to time.

The weight of our packs & equipment is too awful for words. The 5 mile march from the nearest station to here *[ie Monnecove]* almost exhausted everybody.

Will write again when there's more news. Best love to all,

Yrs affectionately R

---

[1] *at Boulogne*: the identification of place names is based on the war diary for the 10th Royal Fusiliers.

[2] *sous*: one sou was 5 centimes.

[3] *estaminets*: establishments which combined some of the qualities of a café, restaurant and an English pub. Found in the villages and small towns behind the lines, they sold wine, beer, coffee etc, as well as simple meals such as egg and chips and omelettes, and provided an opportunity to relax for off-duty soldiers.

[4] *10d*: 10 old pence, 4 new pence.

[No. 9 – marching towards the front – problems posed by the weather, French roads and heavy packs – billets – inspection by General Plumer – Bailleul – Armentières – digging parties – currency]

1st Letter

No Stk 771 L/Cpl RDM
&C
Tuesday *[August 10th]*

Dear Mother,

It is some little time since I wrote my last letter, but I have been waiting until we settled down, & up to the present we have not done so. Letters to-day must be in by 2.30, so I must hurry up with this one. The best way will be to make it a sort of diary I think. I wrote last from the first village we were at *[Monnecove]*. We stayed there until last Wednesday. We got quite attached to it, as it was a clean little place, & the villagers were simple & kindly.

Wednesday *[August 4th]*. We left the village & marched 15 miles. It doesn't sound much, but when you think of the heat of the day, the weight of our packs & the state of the French roads you will understand it was an enormous strain on our endurance. The weather since we have been here has been horribly oppressive, with little wind & occasional thunderstorms. The French roads are horrible. Through every village, & for a mile or two each side they are composed of great rough cobble stones about 8 ins. square & not over carefully laid. Apart from their unevenness there is the difficulty that the nails in our boots slip on them as on ice. Our first casualty was on getting off the boat at Boulogne, when a man immediately slipped over & broke his ankle. If two villages are only a few miles apart they carry them on & join up the two so that they stretch for miles & miles. Our packs I cannot find words to describe. It is a cruel, unnatural weight that no man should be called upon to carry. You get a pain in your shoulders like acute rheumatism after a few miles. The original regulars & the Territorials never carried such packs; we have asked both, & they were surprised when we described ours. They all came over with their spare kit in a kit-bag; but that has been abolished & we carry it all on our back. My pack contains an overcoat, a cardigan jacket, 2 thick pairs of pants, one thick shirt, a housewife[1], 4 pairs of socks, a few handkerchiefs, a holdall with razor, soap, tooth-brush, comb, &c, & a rubber waterproof ground sheet about 7ft by 3 & enormously heavy. We carry an emergency ration of 12oz of bully beef, biscuits, Oxo, tea, sugar &c., a respirator, a towel, a ¼ pint of rifle oil, a pr of indiarubber shoes, mess tin, mug, knife, fork, & spoon, besides rifle (7lbs) ammunition (7lbs) water (2lbs), entrenching tool, bayonet, & often our rations for the day.

Wednesday. We reached in the evening a very small village *[Campagne les Wardrecques]* on the banks of a canal *[Canal de Neufosse]*. We had a swim in the canal, & slept in a barn where there was too much straw. Having had experience of both I prefer too little straw to too much. The country we passed through on the road was awfully boring – long straight cobbled roads with corn on each side, & no hedges. They make the most of the land here.

---

[1] *housewife*: or hussif – a small sewing kit containing needles, cotton, wool etc.

Thursday *[August 5th]*. At 6.30 a.m., still tired & sore-footed we started off again. This day I suppose we marched 11 or 12 miles; & I really don't know how we did it. The sun was blazing hot & the road was cobbled all the way. Every step was painful, & our packs felt simply crushing. To feel hopelessly exhausted & to know you must go on for hours more is not a comforting sensation. The men showed a wonderful spirit, & when on the point of collapse started singing like old boots – which they never do at any other time. We finished at a mere crawl. Only 12 men fell out, most of them going on till they fainted, & several of these rejoined us at a subsequent halt. Unfortunately, of the Battⁿ in front, so many fell out that the Brigade got more or less into hot water. We finished up at another village *[St Sylvestre-Cappel]* & my company were all in one large barn at a very prosperous farm house. I understand the Germans made it their head-quarters last September. The barn was not rat-less & insects were plentiful but it was pretty comfortable.

Friday *[August 6th]*. We remained here all day. The water supply was very poor, & for some days I didn't get a decent wash.

Saturday *[August 7th]*. Headquarters took a fancy to our farm, & we cleared out to another about 1½ miles away. Our barn here was very comfortable. We spent the evening in the village drinking white wine & stout – separately I mean. This was the first time we had come across the latter. The inhabitants here speak Flemish, mostly to each other, but though they understand your French they speak it themselves with so vile an accent that it is difficult to follow.

Sunday *[August 8th]*. I was about to have my first decent wash for a few days, & was climbing up the bank of a pond with a biscuit tin I had filled, when I slipped & put the tin down rather quickly, splashing the water all over me. This made me so cross that it was not until my attention was called to it that I noticed the edge of the tin had cut one of my little fingers & torn quite a large piece out of the other. So again I didn't get a decent wash.

In the morning we were inspected by the G.O.C. 2nd Army *[General Sir Herbert Plumer]*. In the afternoon a portion of each Battⁿ in the Brigade started to march towards the front. We marched about 6½ miles from the firing line, where I was with a party of 40 billeted in an estaminet in the market square. There was nothing very interesting about the town *[Bailleul]*. The roads were in their usual condition. The house we were in was high & rickety, & the staircase narrow & spiral. A family of Belgian refugees occupied the middle floor, & we were above that. We found the floor pretty hard after straw. There was a tremendous bombardment somewhere in the small hours of the morning, the sound of the guns being continuous – somewhat resembling a steam trolley always coming up the road without getting any nearer.

Monday *[August 9th]*. We spent the morning lounging about the town. The cathedral was rather fine, & we heard mass & a burial service. The organ was good & the singing, though queer, being all male voices in unison, sounded very well. Though within range it has not been bombarded. In the afternoon we marched – or struggled – another 9 miles, & are now right up against the firing line. We are in a large town *[Armentières]* rather north of midway between where Dormor is & where our destination was rumoured to be, as I mentioned before we left England. The town has been shelled from time to time & some damage done to the Town Hall & other places. Nevertheless, although some streets are almost deserted, business on the whole is as usual. A number of good shops are still open, & the townspeople might never have heard of the war. We are billeted in a huge place which I fancy has been the "Union"[1], if that is what "Hospice Civil" means. I am up aloft in what appears to have been the children's schoolroom, very long, low, narrow & dilapidated. The place has no end of wings & courtyards, but everything is in a state of squalor & decay with few whole windows. We wash in the "Cantine Scholaire" a notice still remaining on the walls warning the children to "se tenir correctement à table, ne pas de pousser des cris, et de manger proprement".

Tuesday *[August 10th]*. Half the crowd are digging in the day time & half at night – I am with the latter – greatly to my disadvantage, as we get collared for things in the day time & then have to work at night. This morning after a general fatigue clearing the place up we went into the town. The estaminets are closed to troops until 12, there is nothing that takes the place of the English tea-shop, & there was precious little to do. I changed some notes at the Credit Lyonnais (open for a few hours each day, the floor a mass of sand bags & everything heavily barred) & only got 25 Fr apiece – a precious low rate. Later I had a steak & chips – the exact antithesis of a similar English dish, for whereas over there the steak is plentiful, & rich & juicy, while the potatoes are pitifully few, here the steak was a flimsy piece of gristle, but I could not get through one half of the potatoes. In the afternoon I started this letter, but they suddenly wanted letters at 2 p.m. & it wasn't ready. A few minutes later a couple of hundreds of us were suddenly ordered to fall in – we didn't know what for until some hours later, but it was to draw picks & shovels from a place some 10 minutes walk away. We proceeded to what was actually the proper street, but on arriving there the officer evidently had some misgivings about it for we went on for a couple of miles, halted, turned about, wandered through mazes of back alleys & slums & eventually back to the right street again where we got what we wanted, having been 3 hours on a 20 minutes job. However such things are not infrequent. The digging party in the morning encountered a little shrapnel. At night there was nothing to break the monotony. We were some hundreds of yards behind the fire trenches, & a few stray bullets came over us from time to time; but otherwise everything was very quiet. Some desultory shooting of course was always going on, with now & then a big gun or two, & the rockets & star shells were incessant. These are very brilliant & light up everything for a few moments. It was rather a dreary scene – a few deserted or wrecked houses here & there, & the general dismal atmosphere over all.

This morning (Wednesday) *[August 11th]* letters were collected at 10.15, so unless they take more later I shan't get this off to-day, but I shan't add to it. We are digging again to-night I believe.

I haven't heard from anyone yet, perhaps because I have moved about so. Letters seem to be usually about 4 days late. You might remember to add to my

---

[1] *the "Union"*: the poorhouse.

address 111th Inf. Brigade, 37th Divn. I am looking forward to hearing from some of you.

English, French & Belgian money is all current here & it is amusing to discover what a miscellaneous collection of coins one has in ones pocket. English pennies of course represent 10c. or two sous, & a franc is taken at 10d. Thus one has single coins ½d, 1d, 2½d (25c) 5d, 6d, 10d, 1/- & so forth. It is rather handy.

Please circulate my letters as much as possible to save me writing. I intend to number them, so that you will detect it if one fails to reach you. We will call this 1. There is a place "Oliver Williams' Agency, 116 Victoria St. S.W." which is a sort of enquiry bureau, & forwarding agency for the Batt[n] if you should ever have occasion to make use of it.

With very best love to all

Your affectionate

Roland

~

By August 17th, the 10[th]Battalion had moved to Houplines near Armentières. Here it was attached to the 8th Battalion, Royal Fusiliers, for instruction in trench duties.

~

[No. 10 – initial experiences in the trenches – billets in a factory – working parties – army haircuts]

P.S. Please thank H.S.[1] for her letter & explain   Friday, 20th Aug. 1915
I have very little time for writing apart from the   (2nd letter)
fact we can only write 2 letters a week.

Dear Gwyneth,

I have only got time for the shortest of letters, just to tell you what I have been actually doing, without any descriptive adornment. I received your letter a week late, & Mother's 5 days late. The latter is about the average time, so you can work out about when the letters you write will reach me. I don't quite gather from either whether you have got my long letter written from our first billet here, just before we started trench-digging. I said I should number them, so that you would know if you missed any. This is No. 2.

We dug trenches for about 8 nights, including Sunday; starting out about 7.30 & digging till midnight or later. There was very little excitement about it. Stray bullets were pretty plentiful & made you jump at first, & a sniper or two wasted a good deal of ammunition. A shell only came near us once, but in one spot on the way where the road crossed a railway a machine gun used to open at intervals, which livened things up a <u>little</u>. We had two shells in our billets on

---

[1] *H.S.*: Hilda Simmonds, a family friend and the elder daughter of a local clergyman; she would have been about 17 at the time.

different days while they were shelling the town, but neither exploded. The second dropped just as we were going on parade, & it was funny to see everyone standing about in the courtyard bolt for shelter. You hear a shell coming, & it is a thrill better than looping the loop at the Crystal Palace waiting to see where it is going to explode.

The rest of the Batt[n] came up on Tuesday *[August 17th]*, & we moved into new billets. We are now in a factory. My Company is herded up in the gloom of a semi-cellar, where there is a stone floor to sleep on – which is not so cold as you might imagine for to start with you only get about 4 sq ft of it, and secondly the ventilation wouldn't be passed by the L.C.C.

On Wednesday evening *[August 18th]* half the Batt[n] went up into the firing line *[at Houplines]* for 24 hours. I went with this half, so now I have been in the trenches & fired a shot at the Germans. (Their trenches were here about 75 yards away). As we were getting ready to start the Huns began dropping shells in here with more frequency than they have done since we've been here, & as we went by an adjoining factory they dropped one clean into it. The communication trench was in a pretty bad state – nearly to your knees if you stepped into a hole.

We had a pretty quiet time in the trenches so far as the Germans were concerned, for the amount of work makes trench life anything but quiet. A good deal of firing goes on at night, but little by day, as you daren't put your head above the parapet. At night parties go out in front repairing the wire, listening &c. &c. You are awake all night, resting when you can between 10 a.m. & 3 p.m. We came out again yesterday evening. They had been busy at the town during our absence & we passed 2 blazing buildings. We return to the trenches to-night, which is why I have so little time.

I suppose you're at Barmouth. I have forgotten your address. I hope there is someone to send this on. I will write again (to Mother) at the first opportunity. I believe we are only allowed to write 2 letters a week, however.

It's wrong about the Brigade & Div[n] on my address. Please put the Batt[n] only.

When you have a hair cut now you have the clippers "all the way". I haven't a hair on my head ¼ of an inch long. Shouldn't you like to see it?

Very best love to all. I hope you are having a jolly good time. Your affectionate brother

Roland

P.S.[1] There are so many things I have forgotten I must start a new sheet.

Glad to hear you think you will like Bedford. It is nice for you to have Mrs Pacey there.

There were 2 dead German sappers buried just outside my dugout but they didn't disturb my few hours sleep.

---

[1] This postscript is attached to Letter 11 (dated 28th August, 1915) in the collection held at the Imperial War Museum. However, its content suggests that it is part of this letter to Gwyneth (Letter 10, August 20th) and the appearance of the original script supports that conclusion.

I don't know whether you have formed any idea of where I am.

Morris & Fryer have both joined the R.G.A. & 2 other married men in the Dep^t have just joined up. There's hardly anyone left.

I hope this letter is legible. I have just been greasing my boots with raw meat & some has come off on the letter.

R

P.P.S. Please add encs. to my collection

~

After a week at Houplines, the 10th Battalion began to move south in order to take up position at Foncquevillers, some 12 miles south-west of Arras and opposite the German-held village of Gommecourt. (Foncquevillers is the "ruined village" which is mentioned frequently in Roland's letters). Here they relieved the French 355th Infantry Regiment. The Battalion remained in this area until the second week of February, 1916. Their billets were usually in Souastre, sometimes St Amand, and they shared line-holding duties with the 8th Battalion East Lancashire Regiment, 112th Brigade, 37th Division.

~

[No. 11 – spells in the trenches – the journey south – restrictions on letter writing]

(3rd letter)   Saturday, 28th Aug. 1915

Dear Mother,

Many thanks for your long letter, & please thank Gwyneth also for hers. I am jolly glad you are having such a good time, & if the weather is still anything like it is here it must be as hot as blazes. I wish I were with you probably rather more than you do. It must be a bore I should think, the whole place being in darkness after sunset; however you don't seem to complain about it.

I haven't a very great deal to tell you at present. We did 3 days in the trenches *[at Houplines]* altogether, in periods of 24 hours, coming out one evening & going in the next. Then we cleared out of the place altogether & marched back to the town I told you of where before we were billeted in an Estaminet. Since it's all over & we are now a long way away, perhaps there's no harm in my mentioning it was Bailleul. If there is, the censor will cross it out & you'll have to guess where it was. We were in a different billet this time – miles up in a great high building that had been goodness knows what. We arrived at midday on Wednesday *[August 25th]*, stayed until Thursday night & then came here *[Grenas]*. We are now in quite a different part. Do you remember my mentioning a rumour as to our doings just before leaving Ludgershall? It is coming true in every particular, & we are now on our way. The journey was a bit of a nightmare. We left at 10.30 p.m. *[August 26th]* & marched about 6 miles to a railway station *[Godewaersvelde]*. Six miles under present conditions is like 12 used to be. Then at 2 a.m., we embarked – in cattle trucks, as is usual here; 44 men to the truck. We had to sit with our knees up to our chins, unable hardly to move – quite an exquisite torture, until 9 a.m., when we got out *[at Doullens]*, and, feeling more or less hopeless wrecks, marched beneath a blazing sun for about 7 miles to this little village *[Grenas]* where we are now billeted in barns. After a wash down I felt pretty fit however; & just as well, because it took me for corporal of the guard at 6 p.m. This means I have had my equipment on all night & being up every 2 hours to change the guard, trying to sleep meanwhile in a draughty archway – my guard room. I am going to make up for it to-night however. I believe we are here till about Monday.

No, I don't want my letters sent to Oxford. I write there, & to Morris; but not to Vin, or to Waters Upton. You will understand that under the present 2 letter arrangement I shan't be able to write for a fortnight sometimes, but I will send a field p.c. if I can't do anything else. Sometimes I may enclose letters & ask you to post them, as, to a certain extent, this is permitted. Thanks, I don't think I want anything at present, except to hear from some of you as often as you like, & to learn you're enjoying yourselves. With much love to you all, from

Yours affectionately

Roland

P.S.[1] The trenches were infested with rats & mice, but unfortunately there are even less pleasant vermin to contend with. I understand a small bag of flowers of sulphur hung round the neck is a good precautionary measure. If you come across these or know the best stuff to make them of I should like one. The stuff has to be quite fine, so that the sulphur only oozes out very gradually. They can be made double, so that one hangs in front & one behind. Perhaps Mrs Heginbottom has made them for Chum, or some one you come across may know the style of thing. They are used a very great deal here.

P.T.O.
R.

Will you please stamp & post enc^d. I am writing the addressee to get me a watch as I think he can get better value for money than anyone else I know.

∼

---

[1] This postscript is attached to Letter 15 (dated 1st October, 1915) in the collection held at the Imperial War Museum. Although the physical evidence, in terms of paper size etc, is not conclusive, we feel the content suggests that its correct positioning is at the end of Letter 11. We think it unlikely that Roland, on October 1st, would have requested sulphur bags and expressed the wish to obtain a watch, when he had acknowledged the receipt of both, in Letters 13 (16th September) and 12 (7th September) respectively.

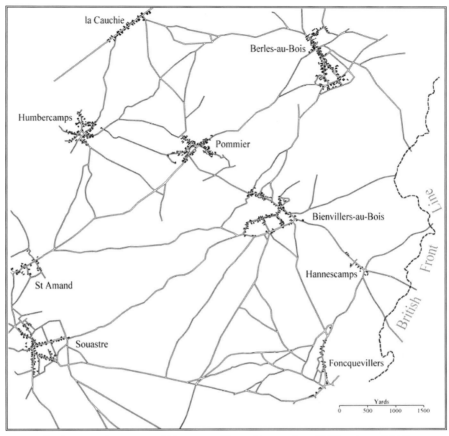

In the trenches around Foncquevillers, September 1915 – June 1916
(Letters 12-37)

~

[No. 12 – taking over French trenches – impressions of Foncquevillers – a disgusting French farm – a jack of all trades]

<u>N.B.</u> I've got the pages messed up; you must watch the numbers.

Tuesday Sept 7th 1915

My Dear Gwyneth,

I have received your letter & Mother's with the views, thanks very much to both. I forgot to mention my last letter was No 3 & this is No 4. I am delighted you have had a good time at Barmouth; but was awfully nervous you were getting horrible weather during the 2nd week. We did here – vile; rain everyday & cold as Xmas. Then on Sunday it changed again & now is glorious – the early mornings (Sept morns!) a dream. Barmouth looks a stunning place from the photos.

The rumour Mother can't remember is only what has happened. You have read in the newspapers that the British line has been extended. Now you can guess what has happened to us. You know Mother's first name. Reverse the letters then knock off the first one. You have the name of the place (almost) *[i.e. Arras]* we are 3 times as many miles S. of as there are letters left. We came up & took the trenches straight over from the French *[355ᵗʰ Infantry Regiment]*. On the whole we don't care for them as much as the last, though the dug outs are very elaborate & the communication trenches very deep & wide. No English, of course, have been here before & we have all the French dugouts & barns; & by Jove, the straw fairly <u>crawls</u>. We came up from a village about 3 miles back *[St Amand]* at midnight last Friday into the trenches, but there was some error, & we only stopped a day & then came back to this village *[Foncquevillers]*, or small town some 1000 yds behind the firing line, in reserve. We shall go up, I suppose, in a day or two, for 6 days. This is now our permanent billet, & we shall stop here doing our spells in the trenches & out until – who can say?

This village (quite a large one, almost a small town) is now a wonderful place. There isn't a civilian in it; or a house that isn't a <u>complete</u> ruin. I haven't seen more than 3 houses possessing more than the outside walls, & perhaps some of a roof. Walking through it you would think that except for a soldier or two it was deserted. I can't tell you how many troops there are here; first because I have no idea, & secondly the censor wouldn't pass it if I had – so you can imagine as many as you like (I don't suppose you'll over estimate it); & <u>every man lives underground</u>. It is a village of human rats. In cellars under the ruins & proper dug outs live – as many men as I didn't mention. There is a barricade every 50 yards in the main street, & communication trenches run off each side & all over the place. I don't mean that we always have to stay underneath. Within certain limits we can walk about – the main street is safe, & many parts of the village are invisible to the enemy; but everyone must sleep underground & when an aeroplane comes anywhere near all the rats scuttle into their holes. We can go anywhere we like looting things out of the houses that are likely to be of any use in improving our own quarters. An expedition of this sort is interesting enough though you see some pathetic sights – lovely gardens with roses & other flowers still growing in the beds, but all run wild or trampled over – large houses all wrecked but still with a few knick-knacks & bits of furniture scattered round the walls; & the church. The church is the most hopeless of them all. The tower is sliced off till it is wedge shaped; but the clock is still there, stopped at 10.30. The roof is practically non existent, & you have to climb a great pile of debris in the centre. A few broken plaster statues lie where the altar used to be, but the walls are quite bare. With one exception however. On the left hand side looking towards the altar is a great wooden cross some 12 feet high with an image of Christ upon it. I couldn't see so much as a shot hole in it.

The place seems to have been evacuated in something of a hurry. One very large house, much more intact than the rest, appears to have belonged to the mayor, or notary, or something of that sort. All his official books are in their places in his office, & the calendar shows the date October 4ᵗʰ.

I & 35 more are in a cellar under a ruined house. Two sides of the house we dare not go round as they are visible to the enemy but there is a small open space at the back we can sit out in. The whole is approached by a communication trench. Two Frenchmen are buried in the centre of the space. They have little crosses, & a proper grave with an empty shell case in each corner. The interior was vile until we cleaned out all the old straw & fumigated the interior. As it is I should prefer the Ritz. A mouse woke me up playing about on my head last night, & I itched all over. We spend all our spare time making what little improvements we can to it.

So now, you see, we are completely cut off from civilisation. It is absolutely impossible, except by post, to spend a single halfpenny. We are wondering how long it will be before we get a drink again.

The place at which we spent one night in a barn before coming on here *[St Amand]* was the most disgusting I ever struck. All French farms are constructed on the same principle = a square, one side of which is the house, the other 3 being barns & outhouses. The whole of the centre, save for a pavement all around, is a heap of straw, manure, & general rubbish. However prosperous the farm, it is still so. It doesn't seem the most sanitary arrangement possible but it is the invariable one. On the muck heap the pigs & fowls & ducks all wander about together. At the place I am speaking of the central morass was particularly offensive; about it wandered dismally a handful of decayed poultry, several of which were featherless in places, & kept falling over from sheer old age. In one of the stables was a white horse suffering from some horrible disease – a skeleton covered with skin & black with flies. A solitary goose emerged at intervals from somewhere or other & paddled in the filth. All the barns were infested with a sort of worm about an inch long, with a long thin tail. The whole show seemed to have gone rotten. Yet a meagre woman with a vinegarish countenance watched us suspiciously all day long from the windows of the house, evidently to see we didn't pinch anything.

In the trenches here we are quite 700 yards from the Germans, & it is safe to look over the parapet in the daytime for short intervals.

By the same post as Mother's letter I received my watch from Mr Clark, a very useful wrist watch, with luminous figures & a strong metal case.

Will you please thank Vin when next writing, for a letter I received from him to-day. I am always very pleased to receive letters, though I cannot answer them all.

It is not permitted to refer to casualties. You must watch the lists in the papers to see how the Batt[n] is getting on.

I don't suppose Mother makes many cakes nowadays. If she does however, I hope she won't forget a small piece for me. As I explained, to all intents & purposes we might be in the middle of the Sahara.

If there are any letters enclosed with this (I don't know yet if I shall have time), would you mind posting them please.

With very best love to you all from

Your affectionate brother

Roland

P.S. In improving these quarters we have had to put our hands to several trades. The number of occupations we shall be able to take up after the war is getting quite large. A little while ago they made us open the seams of our trousers ½ way up, turn them up inside & sew them into knickers. Just as our knees were getting brown they made us turn them down & sew up the seams again. In the trenches at Houplines we had to do all our own cooking. So you see we could make excellent navvies, cooks, tailors, carpenters, bricklayers, waiters, or, at a pinch, soldiers.

R

~

[No. 13 – billets at St Amand – fleas – trench life – a request for 'luxuries' – night watches – an absence of bread]

16/9/15

Dear Mother

I received Dad's letter & parcel while we were in the trenches, your letter arrived this morning. I am rather surprised you have not yet received the longish letter I wrote from our cellar retreat just before going into the trenches, but no doubt you have done so by now. It was No 4 & this is No 5. At the last moment I put 2 letters in to be posted. I'm afraid you'll get a bit fed up if I do that too often, so I won't this time. We arrived back here at midnight last night after doing our spell of 6 days in the trenches. Things are not quite so bad as I anticipated when I wrote my last letter, for after doing 6 days in reserve (the ruined village) & 6 days in the trenches we have come back to this village *[St Amand]* – the one in which we were previously billeted in the farm with the dry-rot I told you of. We are not in the same billet this time thank goodness, though all the places here seem pretty miserable. Last night I was crowded out of the barn & had to sleep in an archway, to-day I have discovered a little sort of cupboard in another barn where 2 of us propose to sleep to-night if we don't find it occupied by geese or something. So far as we know anything of our prospects we are here for 12 days & then go up to the reserve & the firing line & then back again so ad infinitum. There are lots of rumours here, but I don't think much of them. Away north there has been a ceaseless bombardment for 48 hours & I can hear it as I write, still. I don't know what it means.

Thanks very much for the powder sulphur bags. The latter will do admirably, & I hope will be efficacious. I know the fleas don't like it because the other day I found about 17 all round it trying to pull it down a bit lower, as they can't get comfortable in the seams in its present position. Seriously though, I don't believe there is a preparation in existence of any avail against fleas; though I hope the concoctions I have will keep off the greater evil. In our cellar in the village we first came up against the flea as a serious pest. It literally swarmed with them, & after the first night or two no one got much rest. You can't imagine the horrible sensation it is when, just as you try to sleep, you feel them start to crawl all over you. I have sometimes been able to distinguish a clear half dozen crawling on different parts of my anatomy apart from those sitting still, & no amount of powder made the least difference to them. As I heard two men conclude about 2 o'clock one morning, after a long hunt by the dim light of a candle, the only thing you can do is to catch the little blighters. The trenches were fairly free in themselves I think, but we all took a lot with us, & in fact I have some still, though you don't take much notice of one or two after shoals.

There is not much news, as we had a quiet time in the trenches. The only drawback there, if the weather is fine, is insufficiency of sleep. You get 4 hours at night, alternately from 8 to 12 & from 12 to 4; & the rest you get in snatches when you can. If it rains of course, everything becomes a sticky mess & life is a burden.

There is a small canteen here where you can get chocolate & biscuits & moderate beer. For the last 12 days we have, for the first time, depended solely on our rations – a splendid thing for a person with dyspeptic tendencies. Here at any rate you can blow yourself out with a lump of chocolate.

We got the London papers in the trenches from 2 to 3 days old mostly. Today we even got yesterday's.

Thanks for photos which I return. The one with Spencer in is very good of all but the other is too blurred. You & the children are good. I return Gwyneth's & don't mind doing so as I don't care for it. Longing to see you all again in the flesh. Best love. R.

P.S. (Friday) I have had an idea. Twelve days of meal times which left you hungrier than before gave it me. I enclose £2:0:0. I want you, every week or 10 days, not necessarily regularly but just when you happen to be writing, to send me a few little luxuries – a slab of chocolate, a packet of butterscotch, 50 cigarettes, & any little thing that occurs to you. About once a month a pair of thick socks – good sized ones, they always shrink. Keep a little a/c reckoning postage &c. & let me know when the money's all gone. Don't let any parcel (except the socks ones perhaps) exceed about 4 or 5 bob[1] plus postage.

I hope this won't be too much trouble for you. A small parcel means a lot sometimes. In the long night watches in the trenches I simply craved for a bit of butter-scotch or something to suck. I was nearly always up a "sap", a trench going out towards the enemy for 50 yds or more, where you go up at night & listen & watch. You have to keep absolutely quiet, & stay there 4 hours. The enemy here were about 280 yds away, & you could often hear them whistling or singing. Rats & mice came & played under your nose; & the wind whispered in the barbed wire until it sounded like Germans creeping about. If you were on from 8 to 12 there was nothing to see but the Great Bear coming down off his nose & lying down over the village but if it was 12 to 4 you saw Orion rise out of the German trenches, & the Bear gradually get up onto the tip of his tail, & then the dawn broke.

We are absolutely unable to buy bread here – rather a calamity. Biscuits & jam at ruinous prices, the former about 2fr a lb & the latter 1fr for a diminutive pot. Butter is unobtainable, but when we used to be able to get it, it was always

---

[1] *bob*: 12d / a shilling (5p in modern currency).

2fr 10c – 2fr 30c a lb. In Armentieres I once got some Rademakers Hopjes[1] (only they weren't Rademakers, though looking & tasting just the same). I got 4oz for 1s 2½d. They were 5 francs a pound!

There is generally so much to write about I don't know what to select & what to cut out. If there are any items of general interest you want to know, ask questions in your letters & I'll answer them.

There are some rumours about to-day which, if possessing any foundation of truth, mean great things for us.

Best love R

~

On September 24th, the 10th Battalion was withdrawn from Souastre and marched to La Cauchie where it was put on "stand by" during the general offensives, of which the British attack at Loos was a part. The Battalion was to act as reserve to the French 10th Corps. However, the French advance in Artois did not take place and on September 27th the Battalion returned to the front.

~

[No. 14 – a cake received – a blazing barn – Battalion on standby for September offensive – untimely arrival of post – request for goods from home]

Did you work out the letter puzzle? Sunday, 26/9/15
[Line censored] (No 6.)

Dear Mother,

I received your parcel late last night. I see it had been eight days in the post. Thanks awfully for it. It is very kind of Miss Beech to send me a cake & I hope you will convey to her my thanks. It was in splendid condition; the box had not suffered in the slightest. I think if you use as strong a cardboard box always it should come through all right. It is largely a matter of luck. Even wooden boxes collapse sometimes under the strain. Please also thank Mr Heginbottom for the ripping cigarettes which are quite a luxury out here. If I don't have time to write to Geoff, explain to him how I appreciate his kind thoughtfulness. I think the more of the parcel inasmuch as it was despatched before you received my last letter.

It arrived at a most awkward moment, I'm afraid, as you will see when I tell you what we have been doing. We stayed at the village from which I last wrote to you until Thursday *[September 23rd]*, mostly trench-digging, for it was our "rest" & a rest in the army means 8 hours digging a day *[constructing defences at Souastre]*. On Wednesday night we had been in bed about half an hour or so – we go to bed about 8 or half past – when we were turned out to a fire alarm. A couple of hundred yards down the village a great barn was blazing furiously. There was

---

[1] *Rademakers Hopjes*: coffee-flavoured confectionery.

no hope of saving it, so our energies were devoted to the surrounding property. The next barn was full of corn, clover & all sorts of things. Four lines were formed & for over an hour sheaves of wheat & barley & trusses of hay & clover were passed from hand to hand to an open space nearly 300 yards away. I was in one of the chains near the fire end of it, & it was rather a fine sight to see, by the light of the blaze, the long lines stretching up the street round the corner, passing up corn for all they were worth. The sheaves broke or dropped until everyone was knee deep in straw; the flames rose higher than ever illuminating the scene brilliantly & sending Brock's Benefits[1] of sparks all over the village; still the cry was "quicker on the right.". Eventually it burnt itself out & except for 50 men left to clear up the road a bit & guard the property brought out of the cottages we all returned to bed. The next day *[September 24th]* we were supposed to be digging, but the order was cancelled & we received instructions to move at 2.30. We came to a village about 3 miles away *[La Cauchie]*; from which I am now writing – an uncomfortable place, with no straw in our barn, & deep mud everywhere. A thunderstorm broke just after we got here, & it has rained nearly ever since. We are still about 3 miles behind the line; but here we are behind the French instead of our own lot. We didn't do much the first day we were here. Yesterday we went out behind the village to practise a new scheme of attack & were just in the middle of it when orders were issued that the Battⁿ was to be ready to move in half an hour. We were rushed back & packed our kit for dear life. At the end of the ½ hour however nothing happened, & presently rumours of the great things which no doubt you know all about by now began to come through, & we were told we were to stand by ready to move at any time. We slept fully dressed & now it is Sunday morning & we are still here. The official news was read out to us this morning.

It was yesterday evening, when everything was packed up & we were waiting for orders that they took the opportunity of delivering the post which they had been hoarding up for days, so that they wouldn't have to see to the transport of it. Nearly everyone had one parcel, some two or three. We were carrying a day's rations, & no one could pack another ounce; so the only thing was to consume the contents at once. So everybody ate cake to repletion, & tried to give away vermin powder, tinned meat & packets of cocoa; in the end we didn't shift at all.

This morning your letter reached me. It was kind of you to decide to send me things, so I'm glad I wrote my last P.S. & saved you doing it. Thanks for the papers. I wouldn't bother about the smaller periodicals, but a magazine is most welcome. Will you please send some socks with the next one if you haven't yet done so. Please also send with each parcel a 1 lb tin of refills for a Tommy's Cooker, obtainable at Boots. Another fellow has the cooker, & we're sharing the refills. That will send the parcel up a bit; don't cut anything out. I wouldn't send potted meat; but if you can get butter in the small tins we do here I should like that.

---

[1] *Brock's Benefits*: the rockets and flares sent up at night to illuminate 'no man's land' or as signals; Brock's was a well-known manufacturer of fireworks.

I won't write to Geoff just now. I am Coy Orderly Cpl for the week – just my rotten luck – & get continually interrupted. If I can I'll write to Gwyneth. Give her my love. We're a bit sick not being up in the front now. Very best love to all.

Yours affectionately

Roland

P.S. Stk are the distinguishing letters for the Battn, & don't mean anything.

~

[No. 15 – keeping clean in the trenches – casualties – precautions against vermin]

No <u>7</u>   1st October 1915

Dear Dad,

Very many thanks for the parcel which arrived yesterday. You had not received my letter No. 6 when you sent it, I notice. The socks will do admirably, though if there is anything thicker on the market you needn't be afraid of getting them too thick. I have a pack of cards, thanks, & don't need any soap. Soap lasts a long time out here. There isn't enough water to use up much of it. I generally have one mugful to clean my teeth, wash & shave in. I suppose to you it hardly seems possible, but I assure you I do all three excellently. Perhaps it doesn't seem very nice to shave in water you have just cleaned your teeth with, but when you reflect that the water you <u>drink</u> has often a strong admixture of petrol from the tins it's brought up in & obscures the bottom of the mug at a depth of 2 inches you will understand that you're not very particular about what is applied to the exterior. To rinse satisfactorily after soaping yourself well is rather a job, with the half mugful or so that remains, until you acquire the knack. If you have only half a mugful or less to start with, you use your shaving brush instead of you hands, as, although not so refreshing, it does not waste the water so much. With a bucketful the size of a child's seaside toy you can – & do – have a complete bath. With regard to the cigarettes I can do with a large number as you suggest, as I can resell what I don't want. Will you please send the smallest quantity possible duty free. I enclose the equivalent of about 8/-.

I've got no news to tell you. We left the last village *[La Cauchie]* on Monday *[September 27th]* & came up here again *[St Amand]*. I am back in the flea-ridden barn, & we go up into the trenches in about 3 days. We believe we shall attack here, though whether in 3 days time or 30 no one can say.

We evidently made a good deal of row coming in on Monday evening & the Germans heard us, for the village simply hummed with bullets. At the long range & in the dark however, they were nearly all high; & so far as I know no one was hit. We had an officer wounded the other night. He was out in front & they ran against a German sap head: one of the Germans got up to stretch himself & the officer shot him – foolishly, because the rest immediately opened rapid fire. A man who was with him is missing. The last time we were up here another of our officers went back with a nervous breakdown. A man in the machine gun section was blown to bits by a shell just outside his (the officer's) dug out & the shock upset him.

Will you please give Gwyneth my best love when writing. I will try & write her this week. I enclose a note for Geoff, & also one which you might post for me to Hilda S. who has written to me once or twice. I hope you're all keeping fit. Fondest love to all from

your loving son Roland

~

[No. 16 – recent movements of the Battalion – defeating the censor by using underlined words to suggest place names – night time in the trenches – vermin – German shells]

No 8
11/10/15

Dear Mother,

It seems rather a long time since I wrote you more than a p.c., but I wrote to Gwyneth for her birthday & asked her to send the letter (such as it was) on to you. Furthermore, as you said you were sending a parcel last Monday I thought I would wait till it arrived, which it did not do until yesterday. Thanks very much indeed for it. I was glad to get the refill. I am afraid I give you a good deal of trouble though. The café au lait is splendid stuff & you can put a larger tin in in future.

I wrote to you last from the ruined village, & to Gwyneth from the trenches. We did our six days in both places, & then returned here (Saturday night *[October 9th]*). This is not either of the 2 villages we have previously stayed in while we have been in these trenches, but one about a kilo from the one where the fire was. From there we used to march through here on our way to the front. As you may not remember all our various moves, & I sometimes want to refer to them I will give you a short synopsis of our movements since we left the British front. We disembarked from the cattle truck in which we had spent seven hours dolorous *[Douellens]* & cramped & marched 6 or 7 miles to a village where we stayed a week. You remember on arrival I immediately clicked[1] for one of my usual guards *[Grenas]*. Then we marched about another six miles to the place where I described a farm to you. This village was named after a saint, but I should think the heart of the saint ached *[St Amand]* at the amount of filth dedicated to his memory. Then after one day we went up to the ruined village & the trenches for 2 days, returning to the saintly village (but to a better billet) until the day after the fire there, when we moved to the uncomfortable village where we had la cause celebre *[La Cauchie]*, & the sudden half hours notice. From there we went up to the trenches again for 12 days, from which we have just returned to this village, which as I have explained is quite separate *[Souastre]* from the other two.

---

[1] *clicked for*: chosen for. Usually used for something more fortunate – eg 'I have clicked for leave'.

We had a pretty quiet time both in reserve & in the trenches. We seemed to get less sleep than ever this time; but it is wonderful how little you can put up with, & still feel fairly respectably fit. And the appetite you have! Up there there is no use for <u>fastidiousness</u> *[Foncquevillers]*. Here is one example. Every night you can turn in either from 9 p.m. until 1 a.m., or from 1 a.m. till 4.30 a.m. You do each on alternate nights. At nights now they allow a fire in the dug outs, but as we only get enough coke to last 20 minutes for the whole 6 days, the only advantage we derived from this privilege was of burning a few sticks & boiling water for tea or cocoa before we turned in at 9 or 1 as the case might be. By the time you had done this & drunk it, it was usually a quarter to $\{^{ten}/_{two}\}$ so you see you didn't get a lot of time to sleep. Then when you lay down it was rather a matter of chance – you might go straight off to sleep; or a rat might start dropping earth on to you from above, or a mouse try to make a nest in your sleeping cap (I mentioned these pests in my letter to Gwyneth). However I am getting from the point. We were boiling water in a billy can for tea one night when I saw a little chip floating about in it. I asked another fellow to take it out but he didn't do it at once & eventually it stopped in until the tea was made, when we remembered it & fished it out. It turned out to be one of the slugs that crawl about the trenches in millions, & the cup of tea was the best I ever enjoyed.

On our last night in the trenches the Germans, about 9 p.m. sent over 9 sausages[1] in as many minutes; fortunately they were a little to our right, & the next Batt^n caught them. (The next man to me in the trenches, round a corner, is of another Batt^n, & curiously enough a Batt^n of the County of my nativity *[Warwickshire]*). They looked like innocent little rockets coming over, except that they went very high & didn't burst until they got right over onto the other side; but then, my hat! They contain over a hundred lbs. of lyddite[2]; & though 2 or 3 hundred yards away or more, the earth quaked. Some fragments came over us, humming slowly by like great beetles.

This afternoon we have a bathing parade, marching to a small town 4 miles back. I suppose it's a hot bath, & if so it's my first for nearly 3 months. It hardly seems <u>pos</u> *[Pas-en-Artois]*.

One word more & I must shut up. You seem to be inclined to worry about me – there isn't the least cause. There's no sign of anything doing here, & even if there were, there's nothing to get anxious about. I assure you there's as much danger in Piccadilly Circus.

With best love to all.

Yours affectionately

Roland

P.S. I've written this in a hurry, with interruptions & I'm afraid it's a bit scrappy.

R

---

[1] *sausages*: the bomb fired by a German trench mortar, or minenwerfer; hence the soldier's song "There is a sausage gun over the way".

[2] *lyddite*: high explosive; strictly speaking, a British explosive (after the Lydd artillery range in Kent).

[No. 17 – parcel contents – desolation of the forward area – baths – rumours of a rest period]

No 9   Tuesday, 25/10/15

Dear Mother,

Very many thanks for your parcel received to-day, & your letter which I ack^d by p.c. a few days ago. The parcel contained everything I wanted at present. The Hopjes were quite a surprise & are very nice. You can keep sending the café au lait if you don't mind, & in the next parcel I should like more refills if you can get them. Don't worry a lot if you can't though, for I believe you will have some difficulty. If they are readily obtainable I should like them every alternate parcel. I should love the pork pie. Mind it's a good big one. How are you getting on with the wherewithal. Be sure to let me know when you want some more. Don't trouble please to send any more Oxo, as I have quite a good deal now. Will you please tell Dad I received the cigarettes & ack^d them as requested on the wrapper. No doubt you rec^d the p.c. though. I wondered if you would be at a loss to know to what it referred. There were 330 & a tinder lighter. I will let you know when I want some more. I can't think of anything else you can send me, thanks very much.

I was very sorry to hear you had been ill. You don't say whether you are quite well again. I hope you are. I had a very long letter (at present unanswered) from Gwyneth after her birthday. She seems to be in a very decent place; & I should think she will be very happy there when she gets fully settled down. Geoff is lucky to have made such a good exchange, & it is up to him to make the most of his opportunity.

I have practically no news for you this time. I am writing from the ruined village *[Foncquevillers]* where we have been for five days. To-morrow night we go up into the trenches, so I shall be there when you get this. We usually have a pretty comfortable time (considering) in this place, but this time it has been a bit of a nightmare – rotten weather & hard work from morning till night, Sunday included; so that I have had little inclination for letter writing.

Back in our last billet *[Souastre]* we spent most of our time digging, going over 3 times & digging by night behind the firing line at a neighbouring village. That one is less dilapidated than this; though there also the Huns have scored several "bulls" on the Church: but the barrenness *[Bienvillers-au-Bois]* of the country is something appalling. For miles & miles all round here the country is perfectly treeless, except where roads cross it; & along these many years ago a tree has been planted at regular intervals of 50 yards. There are no hedges of course & the cultivated plots where any still exist (and save within a mile or so of the firing line it is pretty well occupied) contain largely roots. Nothing relieves the horrible desolation but the roads striding away into the distance & the villages, which are set in the surface of the waste with a belt of orchards leaving them quite invisible save for the church spire.

We had the bath I mentioned in my last letter, & it was a hot one after all, though as we had to march 4 good miles each way, & when we arrived were only allowed 5 mins to undress, 10 in the bath, & 15 to dress again, opinions were not lacking that it wasn't worth it. You all undressed in one room, & at a given signal rushed into another where there were 4 tanks holding eight each.[1] The previous batches had used the same water, but it was still quite hot & we got some fun out of it, as the tanks only held eight with a squash. After ten minutes a whistle was blown when you all had to get out & run back to the other room to dry (if possible) & dress.

There are various rumours that when we come out of the trenches this time we are going right back for a rest. There is another that there may be leave knocking around in a month or two; but I don't want to rouse your hopes.

I will try & drop a line from the trenches & let you know how we're going on. Do you find our arrangement makes things any more interesting to you? By the way, letters coming out are, I believe, liable to be censored, though I have never heard of one having been. Very best love to all from yours affectionately

Roland

~

[No. 18 – a very wet spell in the trenches – a heavy German bombardment (on November 2nd, resulting in 2 killed and 7 wounded)]

7/11/15

Dear Mother,

I don't seem to have heard from anyone for some time & hope to goodness you are not ill again

I had got as far as the above when your parcel arrived this evening. Thanks awfully for it. The pork-pie was in splendid condition, &, though I haven't tried it yet, looks excellent. The remainder of the parcel is all very welcome. Did you have any difficulty with the refill? Surely you must want some more money by now.

I am quite savage about Hilda's birthday. It just shows the state to which this life reduces the mind. If you hadn't mentioned it I should never have thought of it. I was under the impression I was clear of all such occasions for some time to come. I am writing to her now enclosing 5fr. Certainly we were in the trenches at the time, but I didn't think I would have forgotten it like that.

I was amazed to hear Dormor had gone to Serbia[2]. Have you heard from him from there yet?

Please thank Geoff & Neville for their letters. I will try & answer them.

---

[1] *tanks holding eight each*: the vats in the local brewery at Pas-en-Artois were used to provide bathing facilities for British soldiers.

[2] *Dormor has gone to Serbia*: Roland's brother, Dormor, had joined the Surrey Yeomanry and was sent to Salonika in Greece. Here the Yeomanry became part of the Anglo-French force intended to save Serbia, which had been attacked by the Central Powers. In fact, Roland's letter was written before Dormor could have arrived in Serbia: the first squadron of Yeomanry left Marseilles on November 4th and arrived in Salonika on December 2nd. This suggests that news of the Yeomanry's forthcoming move may have been communicated by Dormor to his parents, who then passed it on to Roland.

You will probably have received by now a letter I wrote to Gwyneth from the trenches in which I said it was muddy & we were having a quiet time. Both statements were inaccurate. When I wrote I didn't know what mud was, & I don't want anything like our last morning again. At Church parade to-day my thanks for my "preservation" were hearty enough at any rate, though I may not have been so emphatic about my creation.

It rained for about 24 hours when we got in the trenches; then it left off & bucked up a bit; then it left off bucking up & then, with a last great effort, finished off with two clear nights & days solid rain. At the end of that time there were places where pure mud came up to your knee, & you nearly pulled your boots off at every step; & the last high water mark left by the communication trench was about five inches higher than that. On our last morning it was still raining, & we were looking forward to being relieved with what the newspaper correspondents call "wild joy". At 10 a.m. I went on for my final spell of sentry duty. I reached the fire trench & had just stood up on the fire step for a casual glance round when a shell exploded on the parapet about 15 yds away, covering me with mud & giving me quite a nasty taste in the mouth. I got down ever so much quicker than usual. Then two more arrived & then several & after that quite a lot. I & my fellow sentry crouched in the trench & wondered if the man who made the rule that a sentry should never desert his post had really thought things out properly; because if not there was a nice short cut to the village. We hadn't decided the point when a certain swishing in the air got gradually louder & stopped & immediately the greater part of northern France just behind us rose into the air with a noise – I was going to say like the collapse of a cathedral; but then I never heard a cathedral collapse, & this may have been louder - & after some seconds descended on us in little bits. I realised at once that I had missed my vocation; & at first wished I had entered the church instead of the Army, but when a few moments later the rest of northern France just in front of me – so nearly in front that my fellow sentry was forcibly induced to lie down on his face in the mud until hauled up again – behaved in a similar manner, I changed my mind & wanted to be an explorer somewhere in the heart of the Sahara. The other fellows were coming out of the dug-outs into the fire trench by this time, the window of ours having been blown in, & two near – one most unfortunately not empty – having been completely smashed in. Then someone shouted "Look out here's another", & I looked just in time to see, spinning round on a wobbly axis, & dropping most uncomfortably near, one of those famous "sausages" you have heard of. So that was what was up, & we began to act accordingly. Taking as much notice of the whizz-bangs[1] & small shell as if they had been gnats, we played a merry little game, the elements of which were that all the players should stand looking up into the sky until one shouted "coming left" or "right" when the remainder ceased to look at the sky & trailed off down the trench in the opposite direction "at the double" (military term for bolting for your life), anybody not quick enough paying a forfeit. After a while they cut out the small stuff &

---

[1] *whizz-bangs*: light shells fired from the smaller German field guns, such as the 77 millimetre gun; their short range and low trajectory meant that the shells arrived very quickly on their target – the noise of the shell's passage and its explosion being practically simultaneous.

confined themselves to "sausages". The bombardment lasted from 10 till 11 exactly, in which hour they sent 60 sausages & over 200 shell. We caught a very unfair share & all the casualties were in my platoon.

At the end we looked an awful lot of guys – covered with mud, faces splashed, & generally fed up. If you want to know what I felt like, I was in a horrible funk, & judging from the faces I noticed, was not unique in that. But such is the strangeness of our national character that we smoked cigarettes all the time – though our hands as we struck the match gave the game away, & made rotten jokes & pretended to enjoy them.

I believe the second period, when we knew they were sausages, was as nerve racking as the first when we didn't know what was happening. None that I saw were as near as those I didn't see (two were within 15 yards & several not much farther off) & I am wondering which way I should have run from these which would infallibly have appeared to be dropping on top of us. Cases have occurred of men running into them instead of away, & I should imagine it's not unnatural either. The blast of hot air which accompanies the explosion is rather rotten, & the row shakes you to pieces. One curious thing I noticed. When one explodes, of course splinters of all shapes & sizes fly in every direction, each with its own note, so that the second after the report sounds like a great brass band.

The wonderful safety of the fire trench as compared with any other part of the trenches was amply demonstrated.

Two days later I went up to the trenches again with a party to see what property had been recovered from the collapsed dug outs. They were firing whizz-bangs up in the trenches, & a few nose caps & splinters flying through the village quite got on my nerves. I don't think sausages have a very soothing effect.

We are back in the same billet as last time *[Souastre]*. We left our trousers off the first day, & went about with our blankets tied round us à l'écossais but it didn't do much good, & they were dried eventually by the simple expedient of wearing them. My overcoat is a fearful sight & isn't dry yet.

It's Monday now, & we have been this morning to have our bath as before *[at Pas]*. We're doing something or other this afternoon, & I can't write to Hilda in time to get the letter thro'. She'll get a letter in a day or two.

Always pleased to hear from anyone who has got time to write. Nothing about leave.

Best love to all,

Yours affectionately

Roland

~

[No. 19 – changes to trench routine – more bad weather in the trenches – the unpopularity of British artillery – poor billets and conditions in reserve]

28/11/15

Dear Mother,

It is ages, I believe, since you got more than a p.c. from me, but I haven't been able to manage a letter. We have just finished our 12 days up at the trenches. This time instead of doing 6 days in reserve in the village & 6 days in the firing line we did 3 out, 3 in, 3 out & 3 in, & I believe in future we are never to be more than 48 hours in. By jove, it's quite long enough too. It's so cold now you get practically no sleep, & the dug outs are dripping water from the roof. You have to hang your waterproof sheet above you like a canopy, & draw the water off from time to time. It also collects all the earth the rats scrape down & saves you from getting it down your neck. The rats have come into their own now. They've eaten all the mice I think, & parade the dug out by battalions all night long.

The day after we got up to the village it snowed to about 3 inches. Then it thawed a little. During our first 3 days in the trenches it froze one day & thawed the next. The three days we were out were very dreary. It froze at night & didn't thaw much during the days, which were leaden grey & misty. During our last three days in the trenches the weather was warmer & still very dull but the rain kept off until the last day when there were heavy showers of snow & sleet.

We had a very quiet time I'm thankful to say. We were shelled very little & never saw a sausage until the last day when they sent about 5 over to the Battⁿ on our right just as we were being relieved; & as I had gone down to act as guide to the incoming Platoon I didn't even see those. Our artillery was very active however & strafed them all day long. We were amazed that they stood it without replying. What it means I don't venture to guess, but it is a fact that in this front our guns fire continually, & we don't get back a dozen whizz bangs a day. It's not like the Hun to take it lying down without good reason.

Incidentally I may say we haven't any affection for artillery. Everything is nice & peaceful & we are just beginning to settle down & make the best of our bad conditions, when the R.F.A, coming leisurely out of their safe & comfortable quarters away back somewhere decide to have a little strafe. So they fire a lot of shells at the Germans. The Germans say well look here we're not going to stand this; we want to be quiet but if they want a noise we'll see who can make most. So they go & fire a lot of shells back. But do they fire at the disturbers of the peace, & try & smash up their safe & comfortable quarters away back somewhere? No fear: they fire at the poor wretch in the trenches, increase the burden of his life; knock down his parapet, which he must laboriously renew, break up his wire, which he will risk his life to mend, & make his leaky dug out leakier still.

We came out of the trenches on Friday night *[November 26th]*, & my Company marched straight back to the town *[Pas]* where we go for baths (do you remember?). One Company has always come here. The remainder of the Battⁿ is in the usual village *[Souastre]*. Coming straight from the trenches the march (8 miles) was wicked. However we did it. Our work here is in the woods. The town lies very low & is surrounded by high wooded hills. We cut stakes, fell trees, make hurdles & burn charcoal. The weather is very bitter. We are in rotten billets open on one side & holes in the walls. I suppose I have experienced weather as cold in England, but it seems very bad. Our boots freeze solid every night; dregs of tea freeze in your mug within 10 minutes; even shaving water starts to freeze before you've finished. A man had an egg in here one night, & in the morning when he cracked it the white was frozen hard, though when fried it was quite good. However we have two blankets & sleep warm enough. I am writing in bed (no doubt you have been wondering what is the matter) as it is the only way to keep warm when you're sitting still.

30/11/15

I didn't have time to finish 2 nights ago, & yesterday I didn't feel like going on. We are having a rotten time here. We parade at 7.30 & don't get back till 4.15 & then we have dinner. Lights out is 8.30. You see we only get those few minutes leisure in the whole day, there are always things to do such as mending & cleaning. The weather has changed completely. It poured hard the whole day yesterday & we got soaked. Imagine woods in drenching rain. I dried my clothes in the obvious way – sleeping in them. To-day has been fine.

Thanks very much for the last parcel. Please also thank the children for their letters & Gwyneth for hers. I can't write to them yet but like to hear from them. You see how it is. Don't worry about not being able to think of anything new for my parcels. The old things are always good. I have missed the magazine lately though. I will send a cheque in a green envelope[1] as soon as I can get hold of a pen to write it with.

I received yesterday a very cheery letter from Vin. As no doubt he will see this I will take this opportunity of thanking him very much for it, & if I ever have time I will answer it.

I forgot to mention that at the ruined village we were driven from our old cellar by incoming water & lived above ground the whole time. Good job they don't shell the village much.

Hope your cold is better. Very best love to everybody.

Yours affectionately

Roland

~

---

[1] *green envelope*: the contents of green envelopes were not subject to ordinary regimental censorship. The writer signed a declaration on the outside that the contents gave no military information. Green envelopes were, however, only issued sparsely.

[No. 20 – mainly domestic]

Dear Dad,

21/12/15

On arriving back at our billet from the trenches last night I found awaiting me your card & Xmas letters from all; also a letter from Gwyneth. I can't write much now, but I just want to write a short note to say how it bucks me up to know you are all thinking of me, & to ask you to thank all the rest for their letters, which I wish I could answer individually.

I shall be thinking of you at 2.39 on Xmas day.

The 12 days in the trenches seemed like 12 years but they're over now, thank God.

I have not yet rec^d your parcel, or the one from the "Citizens".[1]

Be sure & have a good time. I enclose a cheque, & in case you should hesitate to ask for sufficient I leave it blank. Add on another £2.10.0 for my future parcels.

Very best love, & all good wishes. R.

~

[No. 21 – parcels from home – Christmas Day – iron rations – a football match – Foncquevillers church]

29/12/15

Dear Mother,

I don't quite know whether I am supposed to be waiting for a letter from you, or whether you are waiting for one from me. I expect as a matter of fact our letters will cross. The post here has been rotten since Xmas, & I believe a good deal has never reached us. I have not had the parcel from the citizens of Coventry you told me of, & in a letter from Hilda Simmonds she refers to some cigarettes which I imagine she has sent but which up to the present I have seen nothing of. If you see her you might tell her I will wait a day or two to see if they turn up before replying. Your parcel was posted very happily. It reached me on Xmas morning. Thanks very much indeed for everything in it. I am enclosing a note to Mrs Heginbottom, from whom, besides the mince pies, I had a very kind letter. Vin wrote to me, & yesterday I had quite a long letter from Louis. I will take this opportunity of thanking them both (as no doubt they will see this) but I will, if possible, try & write to them direct. I hate not to be able to answer individually all the letters I receive – from the children &c – but I'm afraid it's generally a bit beyond me. I had the usual piece of chocolate from the office, & the assurance of their continued regard for my welfare (which I hope will last until February – rise time), but from Morris I have heard nothing; & fear his & Fryer's letters must have gone astray with the rest. I hear from him otherwise very regularly. He is getting fed up with the Army, as they have twice been told they were going to camp in 48 hours, & then didn't go.

---

[1] *"Citizens"*: the citizens of Coventry – who sent Christmas parcels to Coventry's troops at the front.

I don't know if I told you much about our last spell in the trenches, but whether I did or not I'm not going to say anymore.

We had a very good Xmas day. Church parade was cancelled owing to rain but at 10 a.m. I went to a choral Communion service. I had intended to go to one of the early celebrations but on Xmas eve we were out all day digging just behind the first line in some of the most awful rainstorms I have ever experienced, & all my clothes being wet through I didn't feel like getting into them any earlier than necessary. The service was rather impressive being punctuated by the boom of our heavy guns, which fired pretty continuously all day. At 1.30 we had our Company dinner, the menu consisting of roast pork, potatoes & cabbage, Xmas pudding, mince pies, cake, oranges, muscatels & almonds, beer, stout, port wine & crackers. Not so bad, 3 miles from the firing line. Most of it was the gift of our officers. We had the usual toasts, speech making &c. & on the whole it went off very well. In the evening we had a little festivity of our own in our room. We have hired a room in a house across the road from our own barn & use it in the evenings. I should say "we" means our section, consisting of 10 men. You remember you have a photo of the original section – some 18 men, of whom 6 remain. I don't mean all the rest are casualties; they went sick or took over special jobs & so forth. It gives you some idea of the wastage of a Batt[ns] fighting strength, though.

I enclose a rather interesting cutting – I don't know what from, as it was sent to me from Oxford. The iron ration song is rather poor I think; we have much better parodies than that. At one time they were always inspecting our iron rations & we had one of "Snookie hook'em"[1] that used to start "All day long they call for - iron rations! iron rations! All day long you hear them shout - get'em out! get'em out!" etc. They consist of a tin of bully beef, a tin of tea & sugar & three biscuits which gradually fall to powder or get eaten by rats. I don't know if you have ever met the Army biscuit. It is about the size & durability of a dog biscuit, but tastes slightly better. Since for 3 spells of 2 days each we live on them while in the trenches, it is not surprising that they include the teeth in the medical examination of recruits.

The football match[2] referred to I may have described to you. It was played in this village *[Souastre]*; the "general in goal at one end" was our general, the "colonel in goal at the other" was our colonel; the "captains, majors & chaplain" were ours, the "I" was one of the "soldiers lining the field". I quite agree that I shall probably never see such a game again.

I also enclose a photo of the ruined church *[Foncquevillers]* I have told you of. It shows very well the destruction of the body, but not of the tower, which is much more dilapidated round the other side. It had a narrow escape last time we were up, a "sausage" falling in the church yard. When you see the condition of the building you will appreciate the wonderfulness of the unharmed crucifix I told you of.

---

[1] *"Snookie hook'em"*: a reference to the 1913 Irving Berlin song 'Snooky Ookums', which included the chorus: 'All day long he calls her Snooky ookums, Snooky ookums'.
[2] *The football match*: had been played on October 16th between the officers of the 10th Royal Fusiliers and 111th Brigade.

Except for Xmas day we have had no time to ourselves, digging every day, or else having swank parades with everything cleaned. Life is nothing but getting muddy & scraping it off again.

Best love & all good wishes for the New Year to all from

Yours affectionately

Roland

~

[No. 22 – rumours about future movements – parcels – Winston Churchill]

Thanks very much there's nothing I want in the way of clothes. The weather is very mild. I haven't got a new fur coat, but haven't felt the need of one.

3/1/16

Dear Dad,

Very many thanks for your letter received to-day. Don't worry about the financial mystery, if you can't account for it.

I am delighted to hear you all had a good time at Xmas. I have written since & told you how we got on, & haven't, I'm afraid to say, much news to add. I hope you rec^d my last letter. The post doesn't seem to be everything that could be desired now. I suppose you got the photos I sent?

We came up again on Jan 1st. Everything seems to be much as usual. The rumour of going into reserve for a rest seems to have fallen thro'. There is a new one to the effect that it has been decided these trenches are not in a fit state to put a new Div^n into; & in a way that is reasonable, though rough on us. The engineers say they are the worst in the British line, though I don't suppose they have any means of knowing.

I have not rec^d the parcel you speak of, nor the Citizens, nor Hilda S's cigarettes, nor some I am expecting from Morris. We hear there are parcels back in S. *[Souastre?]* which they won't bring up. We can't imagine why, unless the transport is busy bringing up our new 2nd in Command's hats. He arrived last night, his predecessor being appt^d to a Batt^n. He is rather well known, & as I am not sure whether one is supposed to mention these things I will guardedly say that it is Major W..st.n Ch..ch..l.[1]

I will write a short note to Gwyneth, as she has written me so many letters.

Very best love to all from

Your loving son

Roland

---

[1] *Major W..st.n Ch..ch..l*: Winston Churchill resigned from the Government in November 1915 when he was not included in the newly formed War Committee. Although he remained a Member of Parliament, he announced his intention of departing for active service on the Western Front. For a few days in January 1916 he became second-in-command of the 10th Battalion of the Royal Fusiliers.

[No. 23 – parcels and their contents – Churchill departs]

6/1/16

Dear Mother,

I received your parcel yesterday & your letter to-day. Thanks awfully for everything in the parcel. In my next will you send me the Jan. Nash's?[1] I started the serial in mistake, & may as well go on with it, as it seemed to promise rather well.

Have you had all my letters? I think they must be taking longer than usual to reach you or something.

Thanks for your letter. You know by now I hope that your Xmas parcel reached me on Xmas day. I am most awfully mystified to know what you mean by "The Great Mr Smith" & "Mr Somebody's stomach is better". Were they articles in the "Strand" or something? I thought I read it all through, but don't recall anything like this.

I have no more news as I have written rather frequently lately.

When I was recounting the list of parcels I had not rec^d in my last letter I included Hilda Simmonds' cigarettes. You will probably think I didn't read Dad's letter very carefully. It was an oversight, & I meant to scratch it out but forgot. I wrote her a pretty long letter yesterday. Perhaps if she is staying at 43[2] you may see it. I cut out the mud & wrote about a few details I don't think I've mentioned before. I received the cigarettes from Morris the other day.

Churchill has gone again.[3] Whether he is actually coming to our Batt^n or not nobody seems to know.

Tell Dad not to worry about that money. If it went on Xmas festivities you are not to put it to my parcels a/c.

Very best to all from

Yours affectionately

Roland

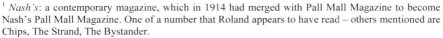

---

[1] *Nash's*: a contemporary magazine, which in 1914 had merged with Pall Mall Magazine to become Nash's Pall Mall Magazine. One of a number that Roland appears to have read – others mentioned are Chips, The Strand, The Bystander.

[2] *at 43*: 43 Park Rd, Coventry – the Mountfort family home.

[3] *Churchill has gone again*: Churchill soon left the 10th Royal Fusiliers to take command of the 6th Battalion of the Royal Scots Fusiliers. He served with that Battalion in the Ypres Salient before returning home in March 1916 to resume his career in Parliament.

[No. 24 – parcel contents – latest spell in the trenches – baths – vermin – a case of mistaken identity]

P.S. Enclose different view   15/1/16
  of church. R.

Dear Mother,

Very many thanks for the parcel, rec^d yesterday. Was there a letter in it, besides the writing on the paper? I didn't discover one. Am sorry I missed "The Great Mr Smith". The article you marked amused me very much. Thanks for the Nash's. I can't think of anything fresh for my parcels unless you put in a couple of soup tablets, which cost 2d or 3d apiece – preferably a vegetable brand.

I'm sorry the photo was taken out of my letter, as I should like you to have seen it. Did you get the photos of the group? I can't get you to say whether they arrived or not.

We got back from the trenches on Thursday night. It was not so bad there this time (though still bad enough) so far as the mud was concerned, but it's getting a beastly noisy place. The only consolation is that they get back about 10 times what they give. We still have to relieve over land, but have managed to make parts of the fire trench more or less habitable. The weather was a bit finer too, which made a lot of difference. There were whole days when it never rained at all. It was possible then, unless you fell over (as everybody does, only some more than others) to keep moderately clean above the waist line, if you were careful always to rub your hands on your trousers. Think of the luxury of having sufficient clean space on your sleeve to wipe your nose on!

We went for our bath to-day. Dad wanted to know how it was we didn't all get pneumonia. I should say because you only undress once a month, so get a nice warm coating of dirt on yourself & your underclothes. I really shouldn't be surprised if there is something in that theory.

Strangely enough we are troubled a lot more by vermin now than we were in the hot weather. I am not so bad, but some fellows are in a shocking state. A couple of them on our sentry post in the trenches the other day disrobed to enjoy the pleasures of the chase. They had slain about 50 apiece when a shell just missed our shelter & smothered them with earth. They abandoned the pursuit.

A man from another Battⁿ came up to me to-day & said he was my brother in law. He said he had been to England & seen my people. I said that was nice for them. He said he had a letter from Ethel. I told him he surprised me. He said he had been coming to see me for some time, & when he was in England my people had told him all about me. I said I was immensely flattered, but was unfortunately a trifle dense, & didn't quite follow how the relationship came about. He explained that my wife had been Miss N or M. I said I was relieved to hear it, as it was one of those things one liked to be sure about. Then he gave me some details about my sister's husband. They weren't very interesting though. I was in a hurry, so when he started showing me some letters signed by one Ethel Mountford I pointed out that, while admitting I was of 9 Plⁿ C Coy, I didn't own that name, my sisters were all children, to the best of my knowledge, information

& belief I had never been married, & that I was willing to bet a fiver he had never seen my people in his life. I left him looking rather blank.

As a matter of fact I believe there is a Mountford at the base, who may have come up with a draft by now, for I have had his letters, but I don't know how the other fellow got my Platoon & Coy.

I enclose a short note to Geoff in answer to his. When does Gwyneth return to Bedford? I'll write to her there when she goes. Fondest love to all.

R.

~

[No. 25 – parcel contents – domestic problems – reading – latest spell in the trenches]

Will you wish Norah many happy returns for me?   26/1/16
She won't hear from me for some days.

Dear Mother,

Many thanks for your letter & Dad's, & will you please thank Gwyneth for a long letter I received from her which I hope to answer in a day or two.

To-day I received a parcel from you. Thanks very much for all the contents. You can keep on with the soup tablets, please; & if you can get brands like "pea" or "tomato" I should prefer them. I'm sorry I forgot to refer particularly to the tea tablets. They are very handy occasionally – but only occasionally so that the two boxes you sent will last me for a long time. The tea that they make is very inferior compared with the real article of course. Coffee & soup are what we live on in the trenches. I hope you will put "Nash's" in my next parcel. I looked carefully through the packing for a letter but failed to find one. No doubt you had nothing to add to your last.

I was very perturbed by the tone of your last letters, especially Dad's. You seem to have many things to worry you I'm afraid. With regard to Gwyneth, she should be the best judge of her chances of getting through the exam from the Bedford place, & if they're not good enough it's no use her stopping there. I don't quite understand upon what terms she stays at this place. Is she paid a salary for being there, or does she pay? Or is it a mutual arrangement? When is her exam? And how else can she be properly trained for it?

As for Geoff, since sending him away from home is rather out of the question, he seems to represent one of the evils that must be endured. He is at a very awkward age – I remember what I was – & will improve as time goes on, but meanwhile it is a great pity that he should be added to your worries. If you think it would be the least use I will write to him.

I don't believe for a single moment you could do better for Hilda than let her learn shorthand & type-writing – or the latter at any rate. There's no doubt she could get into the Prudential, though she might have to wait a bit, & at all events I believe that henceforward there will always be openings for capable female clerks.

So much for all that. I have read Thackeray's "Book of Snobs" twice, though not very recently, once being while I was at school. The second time I enjoyed it very much. I am longing to get back to my little pet library. I have often thought of getting you to send out one or two minute volumes such as selections from Tennyson, or the Rubaiyat, but I don't think I have room for even the smallest, such is our present load. In answer to your query you are quite right to keep on sending a refill occasionally. But you don't always send a magazine. Doesn't the weight permit? You disappoint the whole section when you leave it out. My last Nash's was booked 3 deep before the parcel had been opened 2 minutes. By the way Dad got a word in his letter a little way wrong, & I'm sure with his usual <u>fastidiousness</u> *[Foncquevillers]* he would like to get it right.

I have little for you in the way of news. We had a pretty quiet 12 days out, & came up to the ruined village on Tuesday. We are working the 12 days this time, as we did last, by doing 6 in the village (as we used to months ago, you remember) & the remaining six doing alternatively 24 hours in the firing line & 24 in a sunken road some hundreds of yards behind, where we get a moderate night's sleep in sort of shelters. Forty-eight hours without dug outs proved too much. Unfortunately this sunken road has become far from healthy – shelled daily in fact. They are building dug outs there now, but that takes time. I believe the trenches are improving considerably. The weather of course has been a good deal finer lately. It seems almost possible we may have seen the worst of the winter. There are as usual rumours of going back for a rest, but "as usual" speaks for itself.

I keep well in body, & not incurably otherwise, at present, in mind. Nobody's nerves are a ragged patch on what they were, I'm afraid.

With very best love to all from

Yours affectionately

Roland

P.T.O.

I enclose a cutting you may not have seen. I meant to tell you several times that our reserve Battn is at Leamington[1] – that is the spa referred to. There are several men there I lived with in training in England, who didn't pass the vet. R

P.S. Of course the old Major's[2] there too. You may see him when you're there, one of these days. You would always recognise him from the photo.

~

---

[1] *our reserve Battn is at Leamington*: the 31st (Reserve) Battalion of the Royal Fusiliers was formed at Colchester in September 1915 from depot companies of the 10th and 26th Battalions; it was at Leamington between November 1915 and January 1916, as part of the 24th Reserve Brigade.

[2] *the old Major's there too*: Major White – see introduction to Chapter 2 and footnote to Letter 1.

[No. 26 – parcel contents – the desire for a pork-pie – work on improving the trenches – the arrival of spring – French and German graves – bird life in the trenches – a move anticipated]

8/2/16

Dear Mother,

Many thanks for your letter, also for the parcel. Please thank Dad, Norah & Neville for their notes. I am always glad to hear from anyone who has time to write.

Strangely enough the parcel arrived two days before your letter. The latter only reached me this afternoon, but the parcel I found awaiting me on returning from the trenches the night before last. I was too fagged out even to open it until the next morning. Then, when I woke up & remembered it I anathematized myself in three languages for having forgotten to answer your query about a pork-pie, as that was just what I fancied for breakfast. I answer now, decidedly yes please. Thanks for the magazines. I wish to goodness they would leave off writing war stories. Do you imagine anyone ever reads them? I'm jolly sure I don't. The soup tablets will be sufficient until I ask for some more. While I think of it – will you send me a battery for an electric lamp – ordinary standard size – the flat ones, not the long ones. Thanks for sending Alice's letter. These confounded Zeppelins are getting a lot too clever. I wish to goodness they would bring them down.

We came out of the trenches the night before last. We didn't have too bad a time there. The fire trench after immense labour was thoroughly cleared up & made ship-shape & we even got a communication trench through to the greater part of it. At our end we still had to go over the top but we managed to improve that route a little. The spell of fine weather had a marvellous influence on everything. So the mud wasn't nearly such an affliction as heretofore, thank goodness. But the Bosch[1] is waking up. They have undoubtedly got new & bigger guns behind them here, & are starting to try & give back as good as they get. The result is a horrid noise all day long. Yet I suppose we are lucky, for both on our right & left they have had quite hot times.

Spring is coming on very rapidly. It seems to be a little earlier here than in England. Snowdrops have been out for some weeks & are very plentiful at the ruined village. The graves especially are covered with them. Up there of course graves are everywhere (mostly French) for it was the scene of very severe fighting in Sept '14. In the orchards and in strips of dead ground right up close to the firing line they abound. They nearly all have a wooden cross, some an additional brass crucifix, many the deceased's hat – or hats for often one grave contains a number of bodies. Some bear names of individuals, some the number of men buried there (in one case 112) & their regiment, some simply "Soldats Allemands". They are respected as much as possible but cannot always be left inviolate. Where we have made shelters in the sunken road, as I told you, the

---

[1] *Bosch*: Roland's spelling rather than the more common 'Boche' (or sometimes 'Bosche'); French slang for 'German' / 'a German soldier'.

quick & the dead in one place repose a good deal nearer each other than the former in times of peace would regard as good for the peace of mind. (These shelters by the way have now been removed partly by us & partly by the German artillery). All the dead, however, have not the luxury of a grave, & digging operations near the front line occasionally disclose corpses, which are then given reburial & a cross.

A rather curious thing is the little impression made by the guns on bird life. Thrushes sing now night & morning in the orchards within a few hundred yards of the firing line. Robins have done so all the winter. I have seen owls flying above the trenches at night, where they reap a rich harvest of rats, & a covey of partridges has been out in our wire for the last week. The grass is very long & hides them, but you can hear them often & see them now & again. Isn't it wonderful what use will do? Who would have imagined birds would get used to high explosives? In the trenches the other morning I listened for quite a long time to a thrush singing in the wood behind the German lines. It was a quiet morning & I had never heard anything so impressive as instead of shrieking shells there floated across the wilderness of No Mans Land that breath of old English spring time.

We have seen these trenches for the last time. I can't tell you any details at present for even if I was certain I knew them (which I'm not) I shouldn't be allowed to. When I write next I hope to have a trifle more news than usual. The 10th must be like the wicked for there is no rest for them.

I don't think you need worry that I shall be home on leave before your teeth are right again. Morris has gone to camp at Winchester. They seem to have pretty comfortable huts there – electric light & so forth – & except for leaving his wife I don't think he minds it.

I have not heard from Gwyneth since she returned to Bedford, but I have written to her there.

[last page missing]

~

As Roland had anticipated in Letter No. 26, his Battalion was about to move.

On February 11th, 1916, the 10th Battalion of the Royal Fusiliers left Souastre and moved to new positions about five miles to the north. The Fusiliers marched via La Cauchie and Bailleulmont to Bailleulval, where they relieved the French 2nd Regiment of Cuirasseurs[1]. The trenches were about one and a half miles east of the village. They were to remain in these new positions for just over a month, alternating line-holding with the 13th Battalion of The King's Royal Rifle Corps.

Again, this was a comparatively quiet spell in the trenches and casualties were light. The Battalion War Diary for March 6th said that the enemy appeared "very bored and do not seem at all anxious to look for trouble", although the previous

---

[1] *Cuirasseurs*: originally cavalry (from 'cuirasse' – breastplate) but some regiments were reorganised as infantry.

day they had left a cartoon and message near the British wire showing British prisoners of war gathering the harvest at Doberitz, the "newest British colony", and inviting the British to come and have a drink at the camp! The message bearer had been shot. The incident, however, is not mentioned in Roland's letters.

~

[No. 27 – the move to new positions – return of winter weather – Bailleulval]

16/2/16

Dear Mother,

I don't think I have heard from you since I wrote my last, & no doubt there is a letter from you en route, but it seems I shall have to write when I can now-a-days.

I don't like writing other than cheerful letters, but if I could compose one now I should be one of the most deserving V.C. heroes of the war. We worked very hard on our old trenches to get them in a fit state for handing over, inspired by the thought that we might be going to get a rest. Not only is there no rest, but our task is about four times as severe as anything we have yet encountered.

Last Friday *[February 10th]*, after having been out of the trenches only five days (we usually get 12) we marched 10 miles & straight into new trenches 7 or 8 miles north of our old ones. After 5 months in the trenches 10 miles was a stiff proposition with full kit; & we arrived exhausted. It had snowed all night, & it rained all day – so wet is a mild term to apply to our state. The idea was that we were going to do six days in & six out. A few leaky dug outs, capable of holding about half the men at a time seemed to be the only excuse for a jump from 24 hours to six days. In the summer we only spent ¼ of our time (6 in 24) in the front line trenches. Now, in mid-winter, after six months continuous duty, we are to spend half.

The weather kept fine for a day, & then broke. It rained for two nights; & on the third between 3 & 6 a.m. it surpassed itself. It blew great guns, it snowed till the wet ground was covered 3 ins. deep; it rained again & washed it away; sleet fell & froze as it fell; it rained again & washed that away. In the morning the trenches fell about our ears. In one night the conditions relapsed into those of last December, which I thought were over for good. At the end of four days they relieved us, & we waded out knee deep as of old. We struggled out somehow & crawled to a village about three miles back, the rain still coming down in bucketsfull *[Bailleulval]*. Here we have the prospect of remaining for four days, except for a rumour that we are going in again tomorrow.

17/2/16

As it seems we are not going in again to-night & I feel a bit brighter, I will leave off grousing & tell you a few details.

This is a rather ordinary French village. We have a decent enough barn, with wire beds – a raised framework covered with wire-netting. The village has a name-sake a little way away, except that one is on the mount *[Bailleulmont]*, & ours in the valley. We took the trenches over from the French – a fairly decent lot. On our right the French were not relieved till the next night, so for one day we were in side by side, & since as before, this platoon was on the extreme right of our line we saw a good deal of them. Passing messages down was most interesting. There is –

Post just going. Will write again.

Best love.

R

~

[No. 28 – cold conditions in the trenches – request for further parcels – the German positions opposite]

26/2/16

Dear Mother,

Very many thanks for your parcel, which reached me in the trenches in the middle of the night – the time our post usually arrives there. The pork-pie was excellent, & the other things very welcome. I shall have to trouble you to send me another battery though. The switch of my torch is rather faulty, & the battery exhausted itself in my pocket coming back from the trenches.

I am sorry I had to cut my last letter short. It rained a good deal of the four days we were out of the trenches, & when we returned they were in a pretty bad state. We had a fine day to start with which enabled us to get rid of the water, & then it started to freeze severely, & has done so ever since. On the third day it started to snow. On the fourth it still snowed, & the frost increased in intensity. When we were relieved the returning parties looked for all the world like Polar expeditions, filing laboriously over the wilderness of white. This is our third day out. It has snowed a little every day, & the frost shows no signs of diminishing. I do not remember to have experienced such severe weather in England. A mackintosh with snow upon it will freeze stiff while you wear it. I have a pair of gloves with one partition for the thumb & one for the remainder of the hand. Coming back from the trenches I kept my hands doubled up inside them, & while the upper parts just where my hands were remained soft & warm, the couple of inches spare at the extremity froze hard as iron.

We go up again to-morrow night. This life is rather wearisome. Four days out gives you time to do nothing. First is spent in recovering from the trenches, the last in preparing to return to them, & the other two in working. So my letters I'm afraid will be short & infrequent. I think I owe Gwyneth a letter. Will you please tell her that I can't possibly promise to write to her yet.

I shall be very pleased to get the books you are sending. Please thank Mrs Bednell for me.

If it could be arranged I should like to receive a parcel every time we are in the trenches, as we are more or less cut off from civilisation. We go up to-morrow, ie. 27th – come out 2nd March – go in 6th – come out 10th & so on. If you send off a parcel the day we come out it should arrive early on when we go in again. Let me know when you want money. Cake, butterscotch & chocolate are the main items. The magazine is less important than the food now. Socks every third time.

I'm sorry I shan't be able to write any more on the notepaper you like so much. It was too cumbersome & heavy for active service so I got rid of it. Hope you will be able to read this.

A word or two about the trenches. Opposite us the Bosch is about 500 yards away, but on our left the lines get rapidly nearer, & on the right equally rapidly diverge. I believe they reach a distance of over 1000 yds apart. The ground slopes down quickly from us, so that their trenches are far below. In one place there is quite a steep bank between the lines so that their front line is for a little distance invisible from ours. Behind their line the ground rises again, & we get a good view of their communication trenches. They are in a worse state than ours I imagine, & we have seen a number of Germans dodging about on the top. The distance makes their risk very slight. Close behind their lines is a village which we see distinctly, & shell, too. The line is quieter than the last at present, though I suppose we are here to wake it up. They shell us a little but not much, & their sniping is poor. The latter they can do from the village I spoke of, wherein lies the realest *[Ransart]* danger.

All leave has been cancelled pro tem. The Germans are making a big push somewhere[1], I believe.

Very sorry to hear you have been unwell again. Hope you are all well & flourishing now. Write whenever you can.

Very best love to you all from

Yours affectionately

Roland

~

---

[1] *The Germans are making a big push somewhere*: the German offensive at Verdun had started on February 21st.

[No. 29 – continuing poor conditions in the trenches – changes in trench routine – parcels]

3/3/16

Dear Mother,

Very many thanks for your letter & those from Dad & Neville, which reached me yesterday. Thanks too, for the magazines which arrived just as we were leaving for the trenches. You needn't trouble about sending newspapers. We get them everyday about 2 days old.

The little scheme I told you of for sending parcels to reach me in the trenches won't work now. We came out the day before yesterday after 3 days only, the state of the trenches being so shocking. The thaw started just before we went up, & with the melting of the snow, & the additional rain, & the cracking up of the ground by the frost, the trenches were soon as bad as they had ever been this winter. To make matters worse in the middle of the second day they moved us a couple of hundred yards to the right; & now it takes me about a quarter of an hour to get 50 yards to my dug out. When I do get there I wonder what I have taken the trouble for, for there are inches of mud on the floor, & the water drops from above like a small shower bath.

I believe we are out for three days – i.e. we go in to-morrow night, & it is rumoured that after that we shall do 48 hours in & 48 hours out; but nobody knows anything about it, so all you can do is to go on sending the parcels haphazard as before. You might send the books you mention – they will find plenty of readers. Also please put a pair of socks in both my next two parcels.

I hear from Morris that his wife presented him with a son & heir on the 24th ult[1]. I don't think he expects to be sent out here yet. What regiment is Charlie in on Salisbury Plain? They can come out as soon as they like & give us a rest.

With very best love to all from

Yours affectionately

Roland

Best love to Gwyneth too. Will write some day.

~

---

[1] *ult*: of the previous month (i.e. February); a shortened version of ultimo.

[No. 30 – recent correspondence and parcels – further bad weather in the trenches – Bairnsfather's cartoons]

8/3/16

Dear Mother,

Just a short note to thank you all for your card, letters & parcel. I had the parcel on the 7th you will be glad to hear; it was awaiting me on my return from the trenches. All my correspondence was very accurate. At 10.30 p.m. on the 6th I heard from Gwyneth, Vinnie, Gretta, & Lilly Jones; on the 7th from Aunt Lyd, & parcels from you & Auntie Annie; to-day, letters from you, Hilda Simmonds & Morris. It was delightful to be so remembered, but goodness knows when I shall be able to reply to the whole budget. I am sending Gwyneth a p.c. at present, but will write to her as soon as I possibly can. Neville writes to me very regularly & when I am not so pressed I must write a line to him.

You apparently had not received my last letter telling you of the change in our spells in the trenches. Since then we have continued to do 3 days in & 3 out. The conditions have not improved. The snow I wrote of last time melted, & we were just getting rid of the water when the weather changed again, & it has been nothing but snow & frost ever since. It thaws a little in the day time, but freezes every night, & generally snows some more. Last time up however it was our turn to be the Company in support which was not so bad. This Company lives in dug outs a little behind the front line, & does digging, pumping & so forth. We came out on the 7th, & I suppose go in again on the 10th.

I feel disgusted at the scrappy notes I send now-a-days, but it can't be helped. Hope you are all well, & that your teeth are not worrying you too much.

Very many thanks for all your good wishes, & very best love to all from

Yours affectionately

Roland

P.S. So it was Zepps after all, on the 5th. There are rumours of a rest for us in a few weeks; but they don't seem to be resuming leave. Perhaps they will now Verdun seems to have quietened down.

Do you see Bairnsfather's pictures[1] in the Bystander? He is <u>the</u> artist from our point of view. A lot of them are collected in an issue called "Fragments from France" & are well worth looking at. Cutting out the 9.2's which are always flying about, the idea of things you gather from these pictures is as near the real thing as you will ever get. The small details are always meticulously accurate.

R.

---

[1] *Bairnsfather's pictures*: a serving officer with the Royal Warwickshire Regiment, Bruce Bairnsfather's humorous cartoons depicting life on the Western Front began to appear in the weekly Bystander magazine in the spring of 1915. The creator of 'Old Bill', Bairnsfather's most famous cartoon, 'a better 'ole', appeared in October 1915. The first anthology of his work, "Fragments From France", was published in February 1916 and was immediately successful.

On March 18*th*, 1916, the 10*th* Battalion of the Royal Fusiliers was relieved by the 2*nd* Battalion, Duke of Wellington's Regiment (12*th* Brigade, 4*th* Division). The 111*th* Brigade as a whole was withdrawn for a period of rest, marching via Bailleulmont, Laherlie, Mondicourt and Grenas to overnight billets in canvas huts at Halloy. On the 19*th*, it continued its march, passing through Doullens to its destination of Mézerolles, described in the Battalion War Diary as "a decaying agricultural village on the banks of the River St Authie". Brigade HQ was at Remaisnil and the 13*th* Royal Fusiliers and the 13*th* KRRC were billeted in neighbouring villages. The Battalion remained in rest positions until April 21*st*.

Training during this period was partly intended to "counteract the effects of bad habits acquired through a long spell in the trenches". On March 29*th*, the Battalion was inspected by Sir Douglas Haig and, on the 31*st*, by Lord Kitchener, though neither event was apparently considered worthy of mention in Roland's letters.

~

[No. 31 – the move out of the line – improving weather – drilling – a return to 'civilisation']

25/2/16
[should be 25/_3_/16]

Dear Dad,

I sent you a note in a green envelope yesterday. I hope it arrived safely.

You will be pleased to hear we are having a decent time now. A week ago to-day we left B. **[Bailleulval]** & marched for two days to this village **[Mézerolles]** for a rest. We hope to be out of the trenches for 6 to 8 weeks though not at the same village the whole time.

It is just about a fortnight ago since we went up to the trenches for the last time. The snow & wet had lasted just about a month, but this time Fortune was kind to us. We stayed in 4 days, & the whole time we had smiling skies, with a hot sun & a warm breeze that made the heart rejoice. We got the trenches practically clear inside of three days, & on the fourth sat on the fire step & basked in the sun. After the awful weather we had just come through I can't describe how cheerful the warmth seemed.

Just before we left we had a bombardment of heavy shrapnel for about ¼ of an hour – the most exciting few minutes we have experienced for some time. Fortunately it did absolutely no damage.

We spent four days in billets & then marched off as I have said. The fine weather continued the whole time, even got hotter if anything, & the march was hot & dusty. We spent the one night in huts at a village **[Halloy]** near the one where we passed a week just prior to taking over this line last September *[presumably Grenas[1]]*.

I suppose we are now fifteen miles or more from the firing line, & well off your map. The first two or three days here were lovely. The village lies in a valley, & the slopes on either side are heavily wooded. A stream runs through it, coming down a weir just above the village bridge. We did nothing but lie about on the grass & drink in the warmth & peacefulness among the daisies & celandines. Then as I said yesterday, it turned suddenly cold & we woke up yesterday to find four inches of wet, slushy snow, & it snowed nearly all day. To-day, thank Heaven, it is pure March – warm sun, with wonderful blue skies & white cloud, & a high wind.

We are spending our time at present by doing ¾ of an hour at physical drill before breakfast, & drilling all morning till 12.30, when we finish for the day. We start at the very beginning of the drill book – right & left turn &c. & I suppose go through the whole course gradually doing more each day. At present it suits me very well.

During our second day's march we skirted a very large town *[Doullens]*, from which we are now 5 miles or so. I got then my first glimpse of civilisation for 7 months; & yesterday 300 of us were taken there by motor lorry in the evening to go to a concert. I understand about 20 found their way to the concert, the remainder, of whom I was one, preferred to revel in the luxuries of streets & pavements, & cafés with English beer & stout, & suppers. I am open to confess that my recollections

[last page missing]

∼

[No. 32 – domestic matters – church parade – musketry practice]

2/4/16

Dear Mother,

Very many thanks for your last parcel. Please thank Dad for his two letters, I'm glad he liked his present. As you know I got my reg[d] letter all right.

The peppermints in the parcel were very nice but now the weather is warmer & we are not in the trenches I don't think I should send them again. Some other really nice sweet would be very welcome. Does the 7lb limit still apply? I had an idea they had raised it to 11 again.

I was rather alarmed to hear you had been so unwell again, & hope you are quite better now. I haven't the least doubt you are overworking.

---

[1] *Grenas*: the Battalion had actually stayed there in August but this seems the most likely village.

I haven't much news beyond what is contained in Geoff's letter. Is it a fact that he will be called up? I don't follow these things much – I am rather fed up with what little I hear about the administration of the Derby scheme[1] – but I am under the impression that he has another year to go yet.

I was rather more than surprised to receive yesterday quite an affectionate letter from uncle Bertie. He says that he has heard from Dad from time to time how I have been going on. I wasn't aware that they often saw each other, but if they do I wish you would ask Dad next time to thank him for writing & give him my regards &c &c, & I will write when I can. As a matter of fact I shan't be in a hurry to write, for I have quite sufficient correspondents as it is – always getting slanged because I haven't written to somebody or other; & I shouldn't know what to write about.

He told me about Roy – that he is 16, & at some engineering works. It gave me an awful shock – one of those alarming convictions one gets occasionally of "how time is slipping underneath our feet". I fancied Roy was a little white-faced child – he was the other day anyway.

The weather is a dream – baking hot. Church parade in the open this morning was quite a treat. The chaplain – one of the best – preached about getting fed up. He had three texts, which introduced "fainting" for which he substituted "getting fed up" with rather a curious effect. "Is any man among you fearful or fed up"? or, better known still – "Man ought always to pray & not get fed up".

We fired a musketry course yesterday & with a bit of luck I did rather well – first in the section & somewhere about third in the platoon.

Shall be glad to hear from you when you have time to write, with news of everyone, I suppose at the Swan they are a bit down on me for never having written, but then they've never written to me. Anyway they've got Charlie to tell them about the Army. I heard a man in the billet the other day say rather bitterly "They think a deuce of a lot more about some fellow who's just got a stripe at home than they do of a poor blighter in the trenches".

Best love to all

Yrs affecty

Roland

∼

---

[1] *Derby scheme*: named after Lord Derby, the Conservative politician and Director of Recruitment, and introduced in October 1915 as the number of volunteers began to fall. Using a national register established in July 1915, all eligible males were asked to attest (i.e. state) their willingness to serve if called upon to do so, with the promise that married men would be called up last of all. Once vital war workers had been deducted, the scheme provided less than 350,000 potential recruits and was abandoned in December 1915, leaving the way open for conscription.

On April 21*st*, 1916, the Battalion marched via Halloy to the village of Humbercamps, which was in the same area south-west of Arras in which it had been serving and roughly equidistant between its previous positions at Souastre and Bailleulval. However, Roland did not accompany the Battalion as he had been sent to the Division's School of Instruction.

~

[No. 33 – the Divisional School of Instruction – literary tastes in the platoon]

22/4/16

Dear Mother,

Very many thanks for your last letter. I'm delighted to learn you are better now. My suggestion that you would improve with the weather seems to have been a rather unhappy one, for the weather has changed from being simply vile to completely unspeakable. Thank God we're not in the trenches.

As a matter of fact beyond knowing that we are not in the trenches I don't know where we are. That is to say I know where I am, but I don't know where the 10th Batt[n] is. I believe they moved yesterday from the village where we have been resting to some destination unknown, but I didn't move with them because I had moved already. If you are writing before about the 3rd or 4th of May it would save time in delivery if you addressed letters to me at this address – 37th Divisional School of Instruction B.E.F. I came here on Thursday last[1] for a course, which may possibly last 3 weeks, of general instruction for officers & N.C.O.'s. It was about a 10 mile journey, & I was accompanied by an Officer & 2 other L/Cpls from other Companies. These schools of instruction are pretty common out here; each Division has one, & each Army. There are general courses & special courses such as physical drill &c.

Up to the present I must say I am rather enjoying it. The school is at a large (so-called) Hotel at Divisional Hdq. & we have a dormitory & a mess, not to mention a private entrance to the bar. The mess is a large room in the front of the building with trestle tables & benches; & crockery, with fatigue men to wash it up afterwards, is provided – some luxury for a lance corporal on active service, I think you will admit. In the dormitory are separate wire-beds with palliasses[2].

On the other side of the picture we have severe discipline, unprecedented smartness of appearance, & a long days work. We commence at 8.45 with an inspection by the Commandant, work till 12 & again from 2 till 4, & at 5.30 there is a lecture which does not last less than a hour. On Saturdays we finish at 12 (this is Saturday) & on Sundays there is, so far as I know, nothing doing. The class consists of 10 Officers & 26 N.C.O.s. The Officers drill & work with us, but have separate quarters in the same building.

---

[1] *I came here on Thursday last*: the 37th Divisional School of Instruction was at the headquarters of the 37th Division. In April 1916 these were located at Lucheux, about 4 miles north-east of Doullens.

[2] *palliasses*: straw-filled mattresses.

I didn't know the two other men from the 10th until we came here, but they are a decent sort & we have shaken down well together. That is mere habit, I suppose – which one couldn't acquire in many other ways than in the Army – to live & sleep with anybody anywhere at a moment's notice.

So much for that. I hope you are having a decent Easter. I don't know that it is Easter, for nothing is any different. A man suggested yesterday morning that we ought to be having Hot X buns, & it was only then I realised it was Good Friday. To-morrow I hope to go in to the town I have spoken of *[presumably Doullens]*. We are nearly as far from it as we were before but away on the other side.

Very best love to all & to Gwyneth when she comes back.

Yours affecty

Roland

P.S. Have you read the First Hundred Thousand[1] yet? I haven't been reading much lately, but a few things by W.J. Locke & Kipling's Departmental Ditties which I am getting to know by heart. There are two Solicitors in my platoon of rather aristocratic literary taste, & a Canadian barrister who can speak jolly well, when he likes to do so without quoting Gilbert & Sullivan (which he does ad nauseam on the least provocation), & we get some edifying debates in the barn just around "lights out" sometimes.

R

P.P.S. Monday. Somehow or other this hasn't got posted yet. Your parcel arrived to-day. Thanks very much for it. The weather is better now. Shouldn't know this was Bank Holiday if the calendars didn't say so. Love to all.

R

~

[No. 34 – 'a wicked strafe' – loss of a friend – Amiens – French churches and towns – family grievances – lice – Communion services]

Sunday
7/5/16

Dear Mother,

Very many thanks for your letter, which, as it happened did cross mine I believe. I'm glad to hear you are well again, & hope you will keep so. The weather ought to assist you, if you are having anything like this, for it has been blazing hot for a fortnight. We are still at the School, but expect to leave next Thursday. We shall be very sorry to do so, the more especially now, as the Div[n] is back in the trenches. Our Batt[n] is in them not far from its last position – I think

---

[1] *the First Hundred Thousand*: the best selling book by Ian Hay (the pseudonym of John Hay Beith), which was published in 1915 and described in a fairly light-hearted way his experiences in a K1 battalion.

between that & our former one *[The Battalion was now at Humbercamps]*. In a way I must congratulate myself on being here for the other night they had a wicked strafe[1]. At the same time I feel that I should like to be with my pals if they have got to go through it. I was sorry to hear that a fellow who was in the same tent, house & billet as I through all our English training was killed. We had many a lively night to-gether at Colchester & Andover, & you probably have his photo in half a dozen of those I sent home. I am anxious to know how the rest of them are for we have only had the names of the killed, & not the wounded.

We are still having a good time. The last two Saturdays we have been by bus to a city about 25 miles away – a gorgeous place with tramways & splendid buildings & top-hole cafés. I dare say it mightn't seem so wonderful if it were not so long since I saw anything like it. The Cathedral is very fine, after the rather gaudy style such places usually take here. I must confess that as far as the average village church is concerned it generally rather amuses *[Amiens]* than impresses me. A man in my platoon said the altar always reminded him of the outside of the side-shows at a good Fair, & really I think it a passable comparison. The whole east end is a mass of vile highly-coloured pictures or prints, bits of gim-crack pottery & stupid unlifelike statuettes. I don't mean to say that it is anything like that in the big cathedrals but they have the same tendency. In their case of course the pictures are often valuable paintings.

The porch of the main entrance to this one is all sand-bagged up, although it is so far from the line. I believe it contains some famous statuary. This is practically the only evidence of the war in the town, except for the few English & French soldiers – mostly officers.

I think the most striking thing about French towns is their exact similarity to English ones. Being out of England for the first time you sort of expect to find everything not only being but looking un-English. As a matter of fact the shop windows are dressed in just the same style, there are the same advertisements & notices (I saw "Liebigs"[2] on the side of one tram); I had my hair cut & the barber's shop might have been in the Strand; & there is a market which is as much like Coventry as any others I have seen. It is in the open air, & the stalls are pure counterparts of English ones. The same sort of woman hawks flowers, there are the same variegated & sticky-toffee sweets, the same trinkets & postcards, & the same crowd round the same loquacious vendor who unrolls the same lengths of cheap blouse-stuff, or whatever it is.

You may tell Dad – with reference to the books – that for the last week I have been re-reading the advertisements in an old copy of The Sketch. And by the way what about the April Nash's? As it happened I saw a copy, but that was only chance. I told you I was reading Locke's serial.

What is Dormor doing? Having a pretty dull time anyway I should think! When Gwyneth comes back from Waters Upton I will write to her. She delayed her last letter & p.c. by addressing me as "Pte" for some obscure reason. I was

---

[1] *a wicked strafe*: an intense bombardment of the Battalion's trenches at Humbercamps on May 4th that resulted in 6 killed and 51 wounded, of whom 3 subsequently died of their wounds. 'Strafe' from the German 'strafen', to punish – as in 'Gott strafe England'.

[2] *I saw "Liebigs"*: an advert for Liebigs Extract of Beef, from which beef tea was made.

amused to hear that, according to her, the reason they have never written from W. Upton is because I didn't send them a badge or something, & they saw one I sent to Mill Bank.[1] I never heard of such nonsense. When I was in England I sent or gave anything in that line I reasonably could to anyone who took the trouble to ask for it. I don't know if I was intended to become a general & indiscriminate badge-distributor.

I have been spending the earlier part of the afternoon, like Eugene in "Our Mutual Friend", in the pleasure of the chase; but in my case it was unnecessary to walk about for several hours – I could enjoy the pursuit sitting on my bed. I think pretty well every one has abandoned the idea of keeping free of them now & we confine our attention to an effort to keep down their numbers.

I went to Communion on Easter Sunday. I wish you could see some of the funny little places I have been in for this ceremony. On this occasion we knelt at the little desks in the village school-room. I have also partaken in a tent, in a room of an Estaminet (with a cask to rest my book on), in a cottage, & various other places. A white cloth spread on anything handy, & a small crucifix, with sometimes a couple of candlesticks, form the altar.

Well, this letter is longer than usual, & I must dry up.

With very best love to all from

Yours affectionately

Roland

~

On April 30th the Battalion moved from Humbercamps to Berles-au-Bois, some 2 ½ miles away. It was here that Roland rejoined his comrades after a spell of leave.

~

[No. 35 – a wiring party – leave in London – return journey – the hopelessness of people at home trying to understand trench life]

26/5/16

Dear Mother

Many thanks for your letter & please thank Dad for his. By the same post I received one from Gwyneth. I got them all about 3 a.m. yesterday morning on returning from a wiring party. It rained all night nearly, & the trenches & stores being thick with mud I renewed my acquaintance with that article, getting pretty liberally covered with it. We started about 5 & went out & stuck up a line of wire about 300 yds in front of our trenches. We thought there might be some fire, but it was very quiet & nothing happened. Last night we came in for our *[censored*

---

[1] *Mill Bank:* probably a reference to Mill Bank Road in Wellington, Shropshire, close to Waters Upton and presumably home to some of Sarah's relatives.

number] days, & I am writing in the trenches – the first time for ages, for I never tried to do it at the old place.

I arrived at the office about 11 a.m. on Saturday morning & stopped there till 1. I saw pretty well everyone I knew. I did not hear from Fryer, & have not done so yet, so don't know where he is. As he didn't turn up I hadn't anything much to do, so went straight down to Vin's. We didn't do anything during the afternoon, but after an early tea Vin & I went up west, had a game of billiards (which I won easily) & went to the Playhouse & saw Hawtrey & Gladys Cooper in "Please Help Emily". It was not at all bad. I was in no hurry to get up the next morning, especially as putting the clock on had made us an hour later than France. We went for a stroll, & after dinner I left to catch my train. The journey back was not quite so bad as I had anticipated. We ran straight down to the port of embarkation & immediately went on board. Being early I got into a cabin, & read until we started & then went to sleep. I slept all the way across. We arrived at about 3.30. The French train left at 4.30 (a.m.) & arrived about 7.15 p.m. the journey being much the same as before. We spent the night in billets (rough & bare) & went on at 6.30 a.m. by motor bus to within 4 miles of the Batt^n & then marched.

When I reached the Batt^n *[at Berles-au-Bois]* I seemed to have been away about five minutes.

The thing that strikes me most about it all now, is the hopelessness of trying to realise or make anyone else realise exactly what trench life is like unless you are on the spot. I discovered during the last two nights that my efforts to picture trenches in winter from an armchair at home were about as successful as a blind man's to imagine Niagara. At the same time I was disappointed to find on returning here how little (comparatively with what I had many a weary time imagined) I had appreciated the luxuries of pyjamas, clean sheets, good food, England, home & beauty; having taken it all as a most natural matter of course. From which two things I have arrived at the conclusion that the two modes of life are both natural to me in their place, but like East & West, never the twain shall meet, & it's no use trying to make them.

It rained again nearly all last night, I have a little rat hole of a dug out deep down in the earth. A white fungus flourishes luxuriantly on the damp beams, & a little pet slug does a few tricks just above my head. The trenches are not bad though & I have no doubt we shall rub along pretty comfortably.

I am writing a note to Gwyneth so must dry up. Best love to all from

Yours affectionately

Roland

~

[No. 36 – parcel contents – trench routine – reading matter – tennis with entrenching tools – the "naval affair"]

5/6/16

Dear Mother,

Very many thanks for letters & parcel. There isn't anything else I want at present thanks, except another battery for my torch which you might put in my next parcel, &, I think, a pair of socks. I don't quite know if the literature was intended as packing, or to take my mind off the horrors of war for a few moments – at any rate it was a wonderful selection of its kind. "Chips" is not as good as it used to be in my time I'm afraid.

We go into the trenches again to-morrow night. Last time was pretty quiet, & the weather not bad – two wet nights, but mostly fine days. There isn't a great deal to choose between being in the trenches & out, these days – the latter period including so much night-digging, inlying picquet[1] &c that we only get one or two whole nights in bed. At the end of May they called in all blankets too; & I confess to feeling chilly in the small hours; though beginning to get used to it.

There isn't much news at present. My leave seems a very long way back now. Glad to hear you had a good time while Mrs Owen was over. After all I never went to see Mrs Spencer – forgot all about it in the end. Hope you will make my excuses if you see her.

I have just read "The Amateur Gentleman" by Farnol & enjoyed it; must try & get "The Broad Highway". The small "Rubaiyat" I brought out has been much in demand; its philosophy is rather specially apt out here – except perhaps in the trenches, when you can only "drown the memory of this impertinence" in a limited quantity of cloudy water.

Some enterprising person being possessed of an old tennis ball, our latest recreations are tennis with entrenching tools, on a hard court about as level as a rockery, & cricket with the aid of a biscuit tin & a piece of packing case. After all I don't see why a monotonous dead level & faultlessly turned implements are necessary to sport. You get so many more variations from our method. Doherty[2] himself would have made a poor show on our court, with all his skill.

We are anxiously awaiting the truth of this Naval affair[3], but doubtful if we shall get it until après la guerre.

Hope you are all well & Gwyneth is getting on all right.

Best love to all.

Yours affectionately

Roland

---

[1] *inlying picquet*: presumably, guard duties behind the line.
[2] *Doherty himself*: Laurie Doherty ("Little Do") and his elder brother, Reggie ("Big Do"), dominated men's tennis at the turn of the century: between them they won nine singles championships at Wimbledon. Laurie was considered the better player and is presumably the Doherty to whom Roland is referring.
[3] *Naval affair*: the Battle of Jutland fought in the North Sea on May 31st / June 1st 1916.

[No. 37 – a wet June – a crowded dug-out – Chateau des Rats – Kitchener's death – reading matter and views on contemporary poets]

Will send cheque under   16/6/16
separate cover shortly.

Dear Mother,

Many thanks for your letter received late last night & read this morning, as I was in bed.

What do you think of our lovely June? It might just as well be January – in fact I believe we had warmer days in January now & again. Our last spell in the trenches was perfectly vile. I was on a working party that worked all night & we had one fine night out of six. A wet night at midsummer is no more pleasant than one at Christmas except that it is shorter. It certainly is wonderfully short. On a fine night the sky in the north never quite loses a touch of grey, & by 1 a.m. the approach of dawn is quite apparent.

Apart from the weather I didn't have a bad time. I was first in a dug out called "Chateau des Rats" but more popularly known as "4 by 2". The reason for the former was soon evident – I have never known a domicile more appropriately named. The latter arose from the wire beds it contained ("4 by 2" is the usual term for the bits of rag we pull through our rifles). These beds, except where the wire was missing for a square foot or two, afforded a comfortable couch for the body; but unfortunately the human frame does not stop at that – it has an extra fifty or so inches of lower limb, for which the bed made no provision. I was lucky enough on the second day to find a shelter under the parapet tenanted only by a couple of platoons of rats & a brigade of lice, & to this three of us transferred. We could, at any rate, sleep like men instead of like whiting. As a matter of fact we got rather comfortable there, as it was comparatively roomy. The dug out which I mentioned in my last letter was wonderfully safe, but it held twelve men on the bunk principle – two above & two below repeated thrice; with the result that only three men could get out of bed at once, & even then the place was crowded.

The rats everywhere were worse than I have yet experienced. If you hung a ration bag from a nail in a perpendicular beam & turned round for a couple of minutes, they would swarm up from the floor & down from the roof & attack it front & rear. Any amount of fellows had their haversacks half chewed up. The rats' greatest feat was to kill & devour five kittens nearly three weeks old that the trench cat was rearing in one the dug outs. I don't know why they hadn't done it before unless they were waiting in order to get a better meal.

I suppose Kitchener's death[1] must have caused an awful shock at home. It did not cause such a tremendous stir here. I think the Naval affair, until the truth (or as near it as we shall get) became known, caused much more excitement. The general feeling is that Kitchener has got the war on a business footing, & the rest can now safely be left to his successors. We had a memorial service on the same day as you, but fortunately I didn't have to go. It was our first day out, & the

---

[1] *Kitchener's death*: Lord Kitchener, Secretary of State for War, died when HMS *Hampshire*, the cruiser taking him and his staff to Russia, was sunk by a mine off the Orkneys on June 5th, 1916.

ceremony was held at Brigade Headquarters, half an hours march away, in the middle of a field, & it rained all the time.

17/6/16

The parcel arrived last night; thanks very much. As Dad says, the socks seem rather thin, but I will let you know after I have worn them whether they are too much so.

I am glad to hear you are getting on well with Lavengro. I am not reading anything particular at present – just re-read Thurston's "City of Beautiful Nonsense" & am at present through about three chapters of a paper-covered book with the outside sheets missing, so that I can't discover the author (? ess), which commences " 'Don't be so cynical my dear Elfida' said Lady Silverhampton". I doubt if I shall get any farther. What parcel of books does Dad refer to in his note – Mrs What's-her-name's? If so I received those, & read a couple of them. One of Mason's wasn't so bad – At the Villa Rose. By the way I've just read another of his – The Four Feathers. You see my acquaintance with living authors is being slightly improved by the war. I have looked through an Anthology of modern poetry, & some of it is not half bad, though a good deal is wishy washy enough. I don't care for Newbolt, but Rupert Brooke's "Soldier" is impressing. Bridges is a wash out & so is Chesterton. I haven't got it by me now, so I can't refer to one or two bits that struck me as being particularly good.

The weather has turned a bit warmer I'm glad to say. We go up again to-morrow night. We're only in support this time but it's almost as bad as being in the front line, & not far behind it. We shall be in the part of our front that approaches nearest to the Hun.

I have had a letter from Vin which I answered, but only shortly so if this letter is going around I dare say he would like to see it.

Hope you are well, & very best love to all from

Yours affectionately

Roland

~

*1 Roland in a School production
of 'Julius Caesar'.*

*2 Joseph Mountfort,
Roland's Father*

*3 Sarah Mountfort,
Roland's Step-Mother*

4 Gwyneth Mountfort

5 Morris, Fryer and Roland

6 Roland (right) and Bill Morris on a pre-war outing.

7 Geoffrey Mountfort   *8 Dormor Mountfort*

9 The Mountfort family in Coventry, July 1924 – l to r: Joseph, Sarah, Rex Senson (standing), Neville, Norah, Roland, Frank Spencer, Hilda.

10 The ruined church in Foncquevillers, 1917.

11 A dug-out under the churchyard at Foncquevillers.

12 The Somme Battlefield 1916, looking towards Ovillers from La Boiselle.

13 The track in Sausage Valley along which Roland advanced before being wounded. The village of Pozières can be seen on the horizon.

14 Troops disembarking at Lindi.

*15 Soldiers of the 25th Royal Fusiliers at Dar-es-Salaam,
East Africa, November 1917.*

16 The Monitor Severn

17 Roland in the late 1920s

18 The family burial plot in Coventry's London Road Cemetery.

Photo Acknowledgments

Portrait	*Courtesy of the Mountfort family*
1	*Courtesy of King Henry VIII School, Coventry*
2-9	*Courtesy of the Mountfort family*
10	*Courtesy of the Imperial War Museum (Q2220)*
11	*Courtesy of Pen & Sword Books Ltd*
12	*Courtesy of the Imperial War Museum (Q4123)*
13	*Chris Holland & Rob Phillips*
14	*Courtesy of the Imperial War Museum (Q46406)*
15	*Courtesy of the Imperial War Museum (Q45743)*
16	*Courtesy of the Imperial War Museum (Q46403)*
17	*Courtesy of the Mountfort family*
18	*Chris Holland & Rob Phillips*

Chapter 4

THE BATTLE OF THE SOMME, JULY 1916
LETTERS 38-41

These letters deal with Roland's experiences in the Battle of the Somme. With the exception of number 38, the letters were written after Roland was wounded on July 15th. Letter 41 is the longest in the Mountfort collection; written from hospital in England, it is a frank account of the confused and bloody fighting around Pozières in which Roland's battalion was involved.

The 10th Royal Fusiliers were only peripherally involved in the disastrous opening to the Battle of the Somme on July 1st. Positioned just to the north of the 46th and 56th Divisions, the Battalion tried to assist the diversionary attack on Gommecourt made by those Divisions by releasing smoke over the German positions. In return, the Germans bombarded the Fusiliers' trenches. The main offensive was, of course, further south and the enormous bombardment which accompanied it was clearly audible: "a continual roll of thunder, really awe inspiring", in the words of Colonel White.[1] The attack on Gommecourt was intended to prevent German reinforcements from being sent to the main battle area. Like so many of the attacks on German strong points on July 1st, it failed with heavy loss of life.

On July 3rd, the 10th Royal Fusiliers were relieved of their trench-holding duties by the 1/5th South Staffordshire Regiment, which had been badly cut up in the attack on Gommecourt. Two days later, after the Fusiliers had marched to Mondicourt, orders were received for the 111th Brigade to leave the 37th Division and join the 34th Division (4th Army) on a temporary basis. At 10 p.m. on July 5th, the troops of the 10th Battalion left in motor transport to join the 34th Division in the vicinity of Albert. They travelled via Amiens and Doullens to Bresle, some five miles south-west of the town of Albert, where they arrived on the morning of July 6th. Surplus kit had been left at Mondicourt. On July 7th, kit was reduced still further and deposited in baggage wagons at Bresle.

The following day, July 8th, the 10th Battalion's Commanding Officer and staff reconnoitred the outskirts of La Boiselle village, to which the Battalion would shortly move, returning via Sausage Valley. On July 9th, the Battalion camp near Albert was heavily shelled and a dump of 50,000 grenades detonated. Nonetheless, at 8 p.m. the Battalion moved off up Sausage Valley to relieve the 7th South Lancashire Regiment and to act in support of the 13th Battalion of the Rifle Brigade. The Fusiliers found themselves in exposed trenches and dug frantically to improve their protection against enfilading shell fire from the area of Mametz Wood.

---

[1] Diary of Brigadier-General Hon. Robert White.

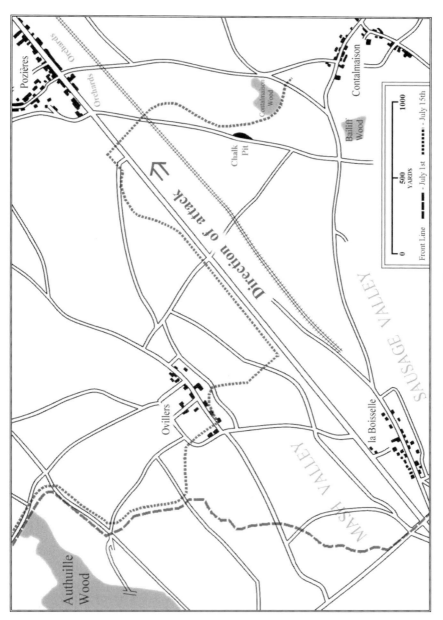

The attack on Pozières, July 15th, 1916 (Letter 41)

July 10th was spent improving and deepening the trenches and burying some of the dead from earlier fighting. In the evening, the 13th Rifle Brigade made their ill-fated attack that was witnessed by Roland and described in Letter 41. They were driven back by machine gun fire and suffered over 400 casualties. The 10th Royal Fusiliers were moved forward to relieve them, with their left flank on the tramway (see map). For the next two days, the Fusiliers remained in an advanced position. Although exposed to heavy shell fire, they still worked to improve their positions and to cut a new communication trench and so avoid having to use the tramway line. On the evening of the 12th, the Battalion was withdrawn to a support position near the big mine crater south of La Boiselle (the Lochnagar crater) and the next two days were spent at rest and digging shelters in the parapet of the crater.

At 9 a.m. on July 15th, the Battalion moved forward once again up Sausage Valley, with orders to support the attack on Pozières. Roland's C Company led the way but, about 300 yards from the village, the advancing troops were held up by machine gun fire. Roland's involvement in the fighting was comparatively brief as he was wounded in this initial attack. After spending about an hour and a half in a shell hole, he made his way back to an aid post. The Battalion's advance had stalled and a sunken road was blocked with troops.

As Roland joined the walking wounded returning to the rear, the Battalion's attack was renewed. A barrage was placed on the southern end of Pozières and soldiers from D Company managed to seize the orchard. However, further attempts to press forward were defeated by concentrated machine gun fire and advanced positions had to be evacuated. Another effort was made in the afternoon but the failure of signal rockets meant that the attack did not start in unison. Despite determined efforts to rush the village, the 10th Royal Fusiliers were again driven back by machine gun fire. After dark the Battalion was relieved by the 10th Loyal North Lancashire Regiment and retired to the Tara-Usna Line.

So heavy were the 10th Royal Fusiliers' losses that they had to be taken out of the line. Colonel White, who had watched the "grand advance" from the Chalk Pit, subsequently wrote that in two days the Battalion had lost 397 in killed and wounded. Although the Battalion was commended in General Orders: "the 10th did all that gallant British soldiers could do", White lamented that "we have paid a terrible price".[1] The Battalion was withdrawn to Albert on July 19th. By that time, Roland was back in England.

~

---

[1] Letter to Captain H.S.H. Hall, July 22nd, 1916.

[No. 38 – the Battalion's move south to Albert (July 3rd-7th) – impressions of Albert]

9/7/16

Dear Mother,

I think I owe you thanks now for about 3 letters & a parcel. I received your last letter last night – the first post we have received for 4 days.

I wrote to you last from the village we were at when I came home **[Berles]**. We – that is to say this Company – did two spells in the part of our line nearest the Germans. It was a curious sensation, after having been so long accustomed to looking over the parapet at any old time, to jump up without thinking & almost seem to bump your nose on the German parapet. Towards the end we got very busy. There was no advance made there up to the time we left, but a series of raids & bombardments. We got a bombardment back every time & things were not too comfortable. On occasions we sent over both gas & smoke. In our time out we had plenty to do.

On the 3rd, after having been in the trenches only three days, we were relieved at short notice in the afternoon. We spent that night in the village, & 6.40 a.m. the next morning we marched away back to a fair sized village about **[censored]** miles away. You can imagine that we enjoyed our evening there for the civilians had been compelled to evacuate the other village, & nobody had had a drink for over a fortnight. It was a hot & dusty march & as usual we arrived tired, thirsty & almost <u>malevolent</u> **[Mondicourt]**. I wonder why fatigue makes people so bad tempered.

[Paragraph deleted by censor]

We just skirted the town to which I went twice from the Div^l School **[Amiens]**, & then we turned left. At this village **[Bresle]** there was a gigantic hut with sort of layers of shelves, like a warehouse into which they put about 750 of us. We stayed there all day & some of the night. At **[censored]** a.m. next morning July 7th, they took in **[censored]** gave us extra **[censored]** & **[censored]**, & marched us about **[censored]** miles to the outskirts of a moderate town which used to be close to the line, but now stands a few miles back **[Albert]**. There was an attack about 10 to which **[censored]**. About midday we moved further up, to the other side of the town, & learned that the attack had been very successful. We bivouacked under tarpaulins that night **[at a cemetery near Bellevue Farm]**. It had rained all day & it rained all night. I slept in a puddle with the rain coming in on me, but slept nevertheless. The next day (yesterday) we stopped there all day, & I am writing from there this (Sunday) morning, but now a hot sun is shining & things are happier. I believe this evening we go up but whether to the support or the front line (such as it is) I can't say. Many prisoners have been taken here, & guns & all sorts of things come down. They say that up in front there's the deuce of a mess of dead bodies.

Yesterday afternoon they let us out into the town for two hours. It is rather badly knocked about, especially the big church – I don't think they call it a cathedral – which is a pitiful sight. At the top of the tower stood a gigantic gilded statue of the Virgin Mary holding the child above her head & this has fallen, but in a miraculous way the base has held fast or caught in something so that now the Lady is in the act of diving into the street at about this angle ⟅.[1]. There are few civilians left & only two or three small shops.

We are surrounded by guns of the largest types & I am almost deaf. At night, besides the row there are the flashes to admire. Sometimes the sky seems almost alight *[Albert]*.

I went to Communion this morning & knelt in the long grass beneath the blue sky. I preferred it to some places I have been to.

Please send a parcel by return with two thick pairs of socks, 100 cigarettes, & as much else as you can get in it. Also some of that Boots' Vermin stuff which I will give another trial. The state of my body is appalling. I believe I could get a bag of three figures any old time with patience.

Please circulate this as much as possible. It's the only letter I've written for about 3 weeks & goodness knows when I shall write another. Best love to all. I can't write to the others but they will understand. Thanks for writing so often. Always glad to hear.

Very best love

Roland

P.S. I think the worst of all this is the waiting. Always "stand to ready to move" & you never know when or where.

~

[No. 39 – wounded]

16/7/16

Dear Mother,

After having been up against the push[2] since I wrote you last, & seen in 3 days more wonderful, more pitiful & more horrible sights than would suffice any ordinary mortal for 3 lifetimes, we tried a push ourselves yesterday morning. I hadn't pushed far before a machine gun pushed a bullet through my shoulder as I pushed up. Am in hospital at Rouen *[missing]* your letter & Gwyneth's the night *[missing]* over. Not much use for you to *[missing]* what is going to happen. *[missing]* love to all.　R.

---

[1] *at about this angle*: the famous golden Madonna on the church of Notre Dame des Brebières in Albert, toppled by German shelling in January 1915 but reputedly shored up by engineers. As Albert was the major administrative and control centre during the Battle of the Somme, the statue was passed by many thousands of British troops. It was always said that its collapse would signal the end of the war.

[2] *the push*: a major offensive involving several divisions; 'The Big Push' was the general name given at the time to the British assault on the Somme in 1916, the term being made popular in the press. However, Roland was already using the term in February 1916 – "the Germans are making a big push somewhere" (Letter 28). The term represented an ideal rather than the actuality and Roland's usage in Letter 39 is clearly ironic.

[No. 40 – arrival in England – nature of wound – concern about 10th Battalion]

> Ward H4
> Mile End Military Hospital
> Bancroft Rd
> London E
> 20/7/16

Dear Mother,

I am afraid I have kept you rather long in suspense since my letter from Rouen, but I have only just settled down.

There is of course a tremendous lot to tell you – so much in fact that at present I am not going to start on any of it – but when I begin to feel at home here I shall have lots of time, I think, to tell you all you want to know.

We were two days at Rouen, & then were sent to England, crossing the night before last in the "Asturias". It is absolutely a matter of luck to what hospital you are sent, & I am afraid mine has not led me into a very salubrious neighbourhood, or the most luxurious of institutions. However my wound should not take long to heal, & then I get 10 days leave before reporting to the depot. We were attacking Pozieres on Saturday morning when I was wounded. Machine guns simply swept our lines, & as I was running forward, stooping, a bullet hit my right shoulder just at the top and came out several inches lower down my back, a nice clean flesh wound. It would be a mere nothing except that coming out at such a small angle to the flesh it has made an open groove about 3 inches long. I have had an absolutely negligible quantity of pain. I lay in a shell hole for a couple of hours, & then, with many adventures which you shall hear in due course, made my way back. I am afraid the 10th will be practically non-existent. We had lost over 200 in the previous three days, & this attack must have about finished them off.

I don't want anything, but you can write as soon as you like.

> Very best love to you all from
> Roland.

~

[No. 41 – preparations for action – the move towards the front – impressions of the Somme battlefield – support positions – the move to the front line – the attack of the Rifle Brigade (July 10th) – German shelling – consolidating position (July 11th) – return to support position at La Boiselle (July 12th) – a gruesome communication trench – La Boiselle and mine crater – the attack on Pozières (July 15th) – wounded by machine gun bullet – the journey back from the front to Rouen and then London – nature and treatment of the wound – concluding thoughts on being wounded – the failure of the attack – medical treatment]

Ward H4
Mile End Military Hospital
Bancroft Rd
E
23/7/16

Dear Mother,

Very many thanks for your telegram which I received yesterday. It was kind of you to reply so soon.

I am afraid if I were to try & tell you all the things it would interest you to hear, I should have a very long job, but I will jot down all the things that come into my head for an hour or two and then when I see you there will still be a little left to say.

I wrote to you last from our bivouac at Albert in the afternoon of the day we went up to the trenches *[July 9th]* – or what there is left of them. We had left our packs behind a couple of days previously & our rig out from then onwards consisted of our equipment less pack, with our haversacks on our back containing a towel & razor, a few odds & ends & the day's rations; a hand grenade in each breast pocket, two extra bandoliers of ammunition slung, a shovel & two sand bags. The attack to which I told you we were in reserve was the first attack on Contalmaison *[by 24th Brigade on July 7th]*; we were too far behind to see anything of it, but as you know it was only a temporary success, the village being lost again later.

We set off at 8 p.m. & went for two or three miles up a fairly good road over the ground where our old communication trenches used to be, through a wood, & emerged into the open country which had been devastated by the advance. There was little to be seen at first, but a mile further on, where trench after trench had been the scene of a conflict it was a wonderful spectacle. We didn't see it that night, for it was dark by then, but we became familiar enough with it later. As far as you can see is a wilderness of torn up soil intersected with ruined trenches: it is like a man's face after small pox, or a telescopic view of the moon. The shell holes overlap & run into each other; some are mere scratches, some would hide an average hay-stack; here and there a few distorted posts form all that remains of a wire entanglement. But the most striking feature is the debris that is lying, scattered on the surface & thick in the trenches. Lots of equipment, rifles, bayonets, shovels, shrapnel helmets, respirators, shell cases, iron posts, overcoats, ground sheets, bombs (in hundreds) – I don't suppose there is a square yard without some relic & reminder of the awful waste of war. More pleasant to behold is the stuff left by the Germans. In their old trenches you can get any mortal thing you fancy as a souvenir, from a sniper's rifle or a grey blanket, to a Prussian helmet or a clip of dum-dum cartridges.[1] If you like you can have the battery that supplied the electric light for a dug out; or the notice board from the one with all the bottles outside, marked "Lager Vorwalker", or the special cardboard case used for carrying explosive bullets. Or you may prefer to collect postcards to "mein lieber, lieber Hans" from "Deine Elise". Personally I took nothing at all. After I had seen dead bodies lying on all sides in the weird attitudes of sudden death, souvenirs seemed a bit paltry.

However, to get on. Our guide lost us – it is not surprising – & we wandered about for a long time in the open, with shells falling unpleasantly near at hand. Eventually we got into a narrow, shallow little trench, where we remained huddled up all night. This was the first support line. It ran alongside what had been a road into a low-lying open space with German dug outs all round it. Owing to their great depth, some were still intact & one was used as our aid post. The other way it lost itself in the open ground for a while. In the morning *[July 10ᵗʰ]* as soon as it was light we were started on burying the German dead who were lying all over the road & in the open square. They had been there some little while, & some were embedded in the mud or half buried in rubbish. I assisted with half a dozen – one we dragged up from a dug out, one from a shed full of German stores and material of all sorts – & then went back and had breakfast. The day was spent in deepening the trench. We were shelled often and had a good few casualties. In the afternoon we saw a fine sight on our right; the second and successful attack on Contalmaison.[2] It was thrilling to see the lines of infantry advancing in extended order despite the shrapnel bursting all around them. They disappeared into the trees, & presently we heard the attack had been very successful. Later appeared strings of German prisoners being taken back.

In the evening we got our first taste of fire in the open. The R.B *[Rifle Brigade]* were holding our front line, & we were under the impression we were to relieve them. The way up was over ground for a little way, then along some trenches, then up a light railway line for nearly half a mile, from which the trenches turned off to the right and left. We didn't know this then but we soon found it out. We moved off in the evening without knowing definitely what we were going to do (our invariable custom) & with many maddening halts & crawls got up near the tram line (I am speaking of C Coy only now). Suddenly we saw that in front they were starting to run. Our Captain stood at the corner where we came out on to the line, yelling "Buck up, they've gone over" & off we went at the double. What was meant to happen I don't know now. What did happen is that the R.B. went over the top to the German trenches opposite them; we came running up the line past the trenches the R.B's had vacated & on towards the

---

[1] *dum-dum cartridges*: split or soft-nosed rifle bullets that would open out on impact, causing horrific wounds; named after the arsenal at Dum-Dum near Calcutta.
[2] *the second and successful attack on Contalmaison*: carried out by the 8ᵗʰ and 9ᵗʰ Battalions of the Green Howards, part of the 69ᵗʰ Brigade.

German lines. The attack ought never to have been made[1] & an order was sent up cancelling it. But the R.B. were already in the German trenches & we were nearly there. We came on, not knowing where we were, where we were going, or what we were going to do when we got there. The Germans of course had got the tram line taped. Shrapnel was flying all over the place and a machine gun on the left caught us with the protection of a bank only about 3 feet high. We seemed to go on for a year. Men were going down every minute, & since there had previously been bodies lying all the way the place began to look a bit rotten. Here and there the lines had been torn up by shells & the holes had filled up with water, so that often we were nearly knee deep & one or two who preferred not to pick their way under the circumstances I saw struggling up to their waists. Then just as I became sure that there was nobody leading us & we should just go running on till there was no-one left, there was a check in front, & the order came down to retire. The advance had been steady enough but I am afraid at first the retirement was a bit of a scramble. It was not for far though, & then we turned, some right & some left into what, as I told you, had been the front line trenches. Our orders were to spread out & man the parapet, which we did. The trenches were being heavily shelled; we didn't know what was happening, & consequently when we saw men advancing towards us fire was opened for a few moments until we saw that some were English. They proved to be R.B.'s, bringing back wounded & prisoners. Of the latter over 200 came or were brought in, & some of them are supposed to have said that if we hadn't fired there was a whole Batt[n] ready to come over & surrender.

That night was rather horrible. We were shelled all night; but the rottenest part was the unsettled state of things. The R.B.'s had now received the order to retire & they came back from the German trenches. (We heard the Germans return to it presently, chucking plenty of bombs about by way of precaution). They were all sent down to our right. (We were on the right of the tram lines). Then they wanted them on our left & we all moved to the right; then they took them away altogether & we were left with about 30 men to a couple of hundred yards of front line trench & had to spread out as best we could. Then they brought up our own B Company & mixed us up properly. This was about 2 a.m., C Company ("my fighting Company" our old stockbroker Colonel used to say) having until then been quite alone. Presently we managed to get some of our casualties away. For some time I was in a bay with one wounded R.B. man lying on the floor, & a man wounded in the throat & making gurgling noises sitting on the fire step. Then a shell burst on the parapet & half buried us all. I lost two men in my section & three from my old section, including Fredericks in whom Gwyneth was always interested. I saw him go down just in front of me in the run up the tram line but he was only wounded I think. (P.S. In this little escapade, which ought never to have been made apparently, the R.B.'s lost all their officers except one, & most of the Batt[n].)

---

[1] *The attack ought never to have been made*: on the evening of July 10th, the 13th Battalion of the Rifle Brigade was ordered to attack towards Ovillers. Although the orders were subsequently cancelled, the news came too late for the Battalion which went forward as originally planned and captured the German third line, taking over 200 prisoners. In the process, however, it suffered more than 400 casualties.

As soon as it was light *[July 11th]*, we started digging down. They then moved us right back to the left over the tram line to get B & C Companies sorted out, & we started digging down again. Unfortunately in the bay where I was, a German trouser & boot protruding in one place rather put us off making it as deep as we should have liked.

We held the front line for two days, & were shelled almost continuously. There were three sorts of shells, a light one nobody minded, a 5.9 which fired either "crumps" (a heavy shrapnel bursting in the air) or a high explosive which burst on the ground & gave you a very nasty jar, & a heavier beast which they turned on from time to time. When this dropped one near the trench it shook your very soul up inside you. Water and rations were brought up via the tram line at night. Of the former we were often very short, & it was thirsty work we were doing. The latter was bully & biscuits. On the second night I was ordered to take three men out & try & get some wire up. I felt it was an honour, but found out that I don't seem to have any great hankering after honour somehow. However we only got up a row of posts & one strand of wire, & then it came on to crump very heavily & we were ordered in. On the third night *[July 12th]* we were taken out, down the tram lines, which were being shelled of course, & back to a support line, behind the one we had previously occupied, which ran close to the village of La Boiselle. Here we were allowed to dig ourselves little cubby holes in the side &, curled up like hedgehogs, go to sleep. It was the fourth night since we left Albert, & our first sleep. We had lost over 200 men already.

Before I leave the subject of the front line there is one little incident I want to recount. The trench to the left of the tramway ran into a communication trench, which led towards the Germans. A party under an officer was sent to explore it. About 500 yards along they found an advanced trench empty, & 20 men & an officer were sent to hold it, which they did until we were relieved. On the morning of the second day I was sent with a party to carry up rations to them. I wonder what the people at home who say "We will fight to our last drop of blood" would think if they were taken up that trench. For 500 yards it is paved with English dead. I don't know what happened, but they were evidently caught there by an awful shell fire – some say our own. In places you must walk upon them, for they lie in heaps. I went up with rations, & again to help carry down a casualty on a stretcher. I won't describe that trench until I have forgotten it a little.

In that support line we stayed three nights & two days *[July 13th – 14th]* & hadn't a great deal to do. For the first time, we were able to make ourselves a cup of tea & we even got some mails up. The village of La Boiselle would amuse you. It is just a broken ring of Bairnsfather trees [1] – only that & nothing more. Not a vestige of anything else rises above the level of the ground. Near here, too, was a mine that had been exploded. [2] I can only give you some idea of it by

---

[1] *Bairnsfather trees*: see before (footnote to Letter 30, Page 68) – the shattered trees appearing in Bruce Bairnsfather's cartoons.
[2] *a mine that had been exploded*: the Lochnagar mine, one of two massive mines detonated at La Boiselle at 7.28 a.m. on July 1st – the second being 'Y' Sap mine, on the west side of the village. The crater left by the Lochnagar mine was some 90 feet deep and 300 feet across; debris from the explosion had risen 4,000 feet into air.

asking you to imagine yourself an ant standing on the edge of a wash-basin. It was in pure chalk, & all the posts & bits of wire, & the whole ground for hundreds of yards around it were white as snow. We slept in our little excavations at the side of the trench, & having no protection were moderately chilly. The man in the one next to mine tried to deepen his a little once & struck sacking. Suspecting nothing he went on & got as far as a blood-stained cap; & then he went to dig a new hole. I had already found sacking in mine, but providentially had stopped there, so didn't trouble to move. What the eye doesn't see &c.

On the third night we knew we were going to move in the morning, & thought that it must be back to rest. The debate on the point lasted the whole evening & we were divided into optimists & pessimists.

In the morning *[July 15ᵗʰ]* we got "stand by ready to move off at an hours notice". As we had been in the habit of standing by ready to move off at 5 minutes notice this looked well. Then at 8.30 we had orders to be ready at 9.30, & then suddenly at 9 o'clock "get dressed". (That means equipment, of course). Nobody was half ready, & from that moment everything was a scramble. We moved off in platoons, overland, towards the front line, jumped over the support lines, & lay down just behind the front line. Then came the order to advance, & before we knew where we were, we were "going over the top". In the distance – a fearful way it seemed – was Pozieres; & we knew by now we were attacking it. Then the crumps began, &, what proved our undoing, machine guns crackled from the village. We advanced at the walk. There was a good deal of shouting – "keep up" "don't bunch" "half left" & so on, but only necessary orders. We didn't dribble footballs,[1] neither did we say "This way to Berlin boys" nor any of the phrases employed weekly in the "News of the World".

We crossed over another trench with troops in it, & about 200 yards further on, as I was running forward a little with my head well down I felt a punch on the shoulder, & lay down in a shell hole to think things over. It didn't hurt much, & I could hold my rifle & it seemed to me I ought to go on. On the other hand I could see the hole just behind my shoulder strap where the bullet had gone in, & I could tell it hadn't merely gone through clothing because my shoulder felt funny. So I lay for some time feeling a good deal of self-contempt, because I knew that if I had the real V.C. instinct I should have got hold of my rifle in my left hand & gone forward with set teeth & a look of grim determination, or else with a strained smile & a joking remark suitable for head-lines.

A man with a bullet through his leg shared the hole, & after a while he went off back. Then a man with a bad wound in the back came in. After a while stretcher bearers, who behaved magnificently, I never admired anything more in my life, came along, dodging from man to man, patching them up with field dressings, helping them into shell holes & carrying on as though it was Hampstead Heath on manoeuvres days; while the whole time heavy lyddite

---

[1] *dribble footballs*: presumably a reference to the attempt made by a platoon of the 8ᵗʰ East Surreys to kick footballs to the German front line during the attack on the village of Montauban on July 1ˢᵗ, 1916. The instigator of the scheme, Captain Billie Nevill, was killed in the attack but the story was subsequently widely reported in the British press and appears to have caught the popular imagination.

shrapnel[1] was bursting overhead & the machine guns were playing as freely as ever. They patched up the other fellow's back & wanted to do mine but I sent them to look for somebody worse. After a while some more came along & as they didn't seem so busy I let them look at my shoulder, & when I saw the back of my shirt & cardigan jacket well soaked with blood I reconciled myself to the idea of getting out of the scrap. I had been in the shell hole for about an hour & a half, but the attack was evidently hung up & the fourth line of our own men had not long since passed over me. So as several times lumps had fallen near me, & I was getting pretty fed up, I took advantage of a slight lull to make my way back to the nearest trench, which proved to be a continuation of the one I told you was full of dead – but here the dead were all German. I got safely down this & along our old front line on to the tram lines. Here again I had an anxious time, but nothing happened until I got near the end, & there I ran into a spot where they were putting over gas shells – not lachrymatory[2] but asphyxiating – & as I had no respirator got the wind up pretty badly. I had not much difficulty in finding a respirator lying about though, & arrived at the open square where, as I said, we had made an aid post in a German dug-out. Here they advised us, if we could, to walk further back, as they were awfully busy & the dug out was full of gas. So we went further back to the next, where they were busier still, & to cut a long story short we eventually walked all the way back to the hospital at Albert. Here I had my wound dressed, got some tea & food, & then was packed off in a motor lorry to some place about 10 miles away, where we got on to some cattle trucks & went by rail to a place called Douras.[3] This was a clearing station. We got more food, & turned in on mattresses in a marquee till 6 the next morning *[July 16th]* when we went by hospital train to Rouen. Tram cars took us to the hospital, situated in the centre of a race course. It was not really more than a clearing station; most of us got blighty tickets, & after two days were taken by train to Havre & went on board the Asturias about 9 p.m. Tuesday night *[July 18th]*. It was very crowded, no beds left & we slept on the mess room floor. At Southampton next morning I missed by a fluke a train going to Carlisle or some impossible place & the next one happened to be London. At Waterloo I was with the first party of 30 out of the train & they put us into private cars. I saw a nurse give the driver a card with Mile End on it, & knew our fate. There was the fatheaded crowd, just as you read of, gaping & throwing cigarettes &c & the whole ride was most detestable – through the heart of London with me perched up in front, not quite in such a bad state as on reaching Rouen, but nevertheless with two days dirt & beard, hatless & dishevelled, & a dangling sleeve.

I dare say you are getting tired of this, & I know I am, so will leave a few remarks about the hospital itself until I write again. Its great redeeming feature is that anyone who is well enough to do it can go out on Mon. Tue. Fri. & Saty from 1 till 6, so I intend to have as good a time as I can. I have already been to the office, & much to my disgust was dragged all over the place, even to the Asst.

---

[1] *shrapnel*: shells which burst in the air and rained down lead balls that had been packed within the shells. (Also the pieces of metal from exploding shells).

[2] *not lachrymatory*: i.e. not tear gas.

[3] *Douras*: no place of that name exists but a Casualty Clearing Station had been established at Daours in May 1916. Daours is just east of Amiens and on the railway line from Albert.

Managers, quite exalted persons before whom I should have stood & trembled in the old days, but with whom in my new position I had quite a familiar conversation. I can't say I like parading London in a uniform of various blues with an offensive red tie;[1] but perhaps I shall get used to it.

My wound is dressed twice a day, & is more painful every time – a sign, as I am assured, that it is healing up nicely. It has to be "packed" at the lower entrance, which means that a few yards of bandage are poked up with a knitting needle, to keep it open & allow it to discharge. It consists of a little blue mark on the top of my shoulder where the bullet went in, & a long deep slit a few inches down my back where it came out. Possibly it turned a little in its course. The official diagnosis on my sheet is "Gun shot. Small entry wound above right clavicle; large furrowed wound on scapular muscles at exit." It doesn't interfere to any great extent with the use of my right arm so long as my shoulder muscles are not involved.

It was kind of you to write to Auntie Annie; she seems to have appreciated it very much. They are very concerned just now about Vernon's wife, who is in a Home, & doesn't seem to be progressing very favourably.

I hope to be seeing Vin very shortly. At present he is confined to the house with a displaced cartilage in the knee, he tells me.

Very best love to all. It is good to think I shall be seeing you all before long. Hope you are all well. Any particular troubles at present? Again best love.

Roland

P.S. Many happy returns of the 25th. What do you fancy for a present?   R.

P.P.S. Three things have occurred to me on reading this over which I may as well get down before turning in.

1. I can remember now what a curious feeling it gave me to be leaving my equipment behind; even at that time & place. There was my rifle, on which for more than 12 months I have spent hours & hours of labour to keep clean, looked after better than myself often; fixed bayonet, one cartridge in the chamber, cocked & safety catch on. My equipment I have greased & polished many a hundred times, my ammunition, all laboriously cleaned a few days before; iron rations, until then clung to like life itself; ground sheet, haversack, with razor from Hadden's, brush from Leytonstone years ago – & all my portable property that I had carried until it seemed almost part of me – chucked into a shell hole & left there to rot.

2. I gather the attack was a failure. The latest I can be sure of is that we reached a trench just in front of the village, & finding it useless to go on, lay there until 6 p.m. while the artillery had another go. This trench was so full that 9 & 12 platoons had to lie behind the parados.[2] One man said he could only see 5 men of

---

[1] *uniform of various blues with an offensive red tie*: the blue uniform and accompanying red tie issued to convalescent soldiers in the UK.
[2] *parados*: the raised section of sandbags at the back of the trench. i.e. the part furthest away from the enemy.

9 platoon. At 6 p.m. they advanced, & I have met no one who knows what happened. But the papers never said a word about the affair, so I gather it was a complete failure. One man thought we had had to retire right back to our original position. I trust it was not so or many wounded would have been left lying out. (The men who held the advanced trench I told you of said that at night you could hear wounded out in front crying for help & water, but nothing could be done). Two brigades were employed, & the dead & wounded were thick as peas. I have written to my platoon officer to know who is left.

The failure seems to me to have been due to insufficient artillery preparation (why Heaven only knows for we had enough in all conscience; Albert bristled with guns of all calibres) & a too lengthy advance. It was too much to try. I must have gone 500 yards before I went down, & the village still seemed a long way.

3. The treatment we got in French hospital trains & hospitals was greatly superior to that over here; but of course we had a good deal more experience of them. This hospital & the journey here from Southampton was all we saw of this side, but neither is anything to be proud of, after the way they do things over there.

R.

~

Chapter 5

LONDON, AUGUST – SEPTEMBER 1916
LETTERS 42-48

Letters 42 – 48 are written from Mile End Hospital in London during Roland's recuperation from the gunshot wound he received on the Somme. Although not too serious, the wound was still "one of the largest in the minor cases" and took time to heal. Literature and outings to London's revues provided some consolation for the boredom of life in hospital. He also drew comfort from being away from the front: "to leave here means to go back to France ... The end of the war seems to be the only thing worth looking forward to."

During this time Roland learnt of comrades who had also become casualties during the Battle of the Somme. These included two of his closest friends who had died as a result of the fighting: "We three were together during all the bad times at the end, & since they were both much cleverer & more useful individuals than I, I don't think the selection a good one."

~

[No. 42 – likely loss of Pickering and other friends – views on the 'Compleat Angler' – other reading – suggestions for making tea]

Ward H4
Mile End Mily
Hosp[1]
Bancroft Rd E
2/8/16

Dear Mother,

I haven't much to say but there is still an hour to bed-time, & I have been perseveringly doing nothing all day; with the result that I feel very limp & vacant, & think something ought to be done about it.

I have had bad news today, though only such as I might have expected. The first letters have arrived from France, & though they say very little about what I want to know, it seems that two of my best friends have not been heard of and are believed to have been killed. Of Pickering I can't hear a word. I am inclined to think from this that he is either killed or wounded, for I know he was the next for promotion, & the new N.C.O.'s in the platoon do not include him among their number.[1] This number by the way, for No 9 Platoon alone comprises two l/cpls promoted to be sergts & 4 privates to l/cpls, so the toll of N.C.O.'s seems to have been heavy. I am waiting to hear more definite news, which I hope will be better. One of the fellows I speak of was a solicitor from Yorkshire. We had many tastes in common, but also many in contrast; which is just as it should be. We "spoke with naked hearts together" & had sometimes cut in half our last cigarette. The other was a little fellow[2] – a most delightful companion, full of humour & good spirits. We three were together during all the bad times at the end, & since they were both much cleverer & more useful individuals than I, I don't think the selection a good one.

<u>Thursday evening</u>

I didn't get far last night, as you see, but fell into a reverie till bed-time. It is just the same time to-night, & I have spent the day in much the same way.

With reference to the Compleat Angler. I enjoyed parts of it very much. I got rather bored with the Fourth day where chapter after chapter is merely a string of facts about various kinds of fish. In places your breath is quite taken away by the rapidity with which events happen. He uses no asterisks or dashes & three sentences apparently spoken in one breath carry you from the river to supper & from supper to bed. But what struck me most was the extraordinary combination of knowledge & ignorance that the author shows when he treats of natural history. He could give the life history in detail of nearly every fresh water fish that swims, & yet could say that "it is not to be doubted" that some pike are bred by the pickerel weed "& other glutinous matter, with the help of the sun's heat" & that "eels may be bred as some worms, & some kinds of bees & wasps are, either of dew, or out of the corruption of the earth" adducing in evidence that "barnacles & young goslings are bred by the sun's heat & the rotten planks of an old ship". Similarly, though he was so intimate with various kinds of grubs, & the place to seek them, he knew little about their existence. He evidently once found a privet caterpillar, but could only suggest that "doubtless it turned to one of those flies of prey." Some of his expressions are very quaint. I laughed at his description of the palmer worm that won't feed on one plant but will "boldly & disorderly wander up & down" and conjured up a mental picture of a lawless & uproarious palmer worm arrested by a couple of stag-beetles, confined in an arum-lily & charged with wandering up & down in a disorderly manner. The quality of the poetry he quotes varies a good deal, but some of it is rather fine, particularly, in my opinion, the last piece in the book. He gives (unconsciously) a good example of a superstition which is by no means extinct at the present day, that the more difficult an article is to obtain, the greater virtue it possesses when used, in stating that a bait will be more efficacious if anointed with "the marrow of the thigh bone of a heron". Well, so much for Izaak. I have also been reading "The Autocrat of the Breakfast Table"; "The Atheist's Mass" & other short stories by Balzac;

---

[1] *do not include him among their number*: Roland's fears were soon confirmed: Private STK/792 Ernest A. Pickering had died of wounds on Monday, July 17th, at the age of 29 years. He is buried in Abbeville Communal Cemetery on the Somme. See Letter 45.

[2] *a little fellow*: presumably Ernest Pickering, who had been born in London; the identity of the 'solicitor from Yorkshire' is unknown.

Poems by John Masefield; "A Man's Man" (Ian Hay), "The Broad Highway" &c. I can recommend them all (except perhaps the Poems), if you haven't read some of them. I am about to start on "Mrs Skaggs Husband" & other sketches & tales by Bret Harte; & after that I don't quite know what to turn to.

I rec.^d your letter yesterday (it's Friday morning now). I was surprised to hear you expected me this week. A fortnight from when I wrote last is the lowest estimate. It is healing tremendously fast; but it was a large wound – one of the largest in the "minor cases" side of the hospital. I hope you don't think I came home with a scratch.

I enclose a chq. which Dad will cash for you. It had come to my knowledge that you were rather wanting some contrivance to enable you to make an early cup of tea in the bed room, so I had a look round to see what was doing, but didn't see much. I had an idea though, that you may think worth considering. It seems to me far & away the best scheme. Get a Thermos flask, & when you are making tea the afternoon before, make a little extra & fill it; then in the morning all you have to do is to pour it out; & if it is a good flask it will be near enough as hot as when you put it in.

Please thank Gwyneth for her note. I hope you are all well. Best love to all from

Yours affectionately

Roland

~

[No. 43 – time in London – recent reading – domestic matters – a missing parcel]

Mile End
7/8/16

Dear Mother,

Many thanks for your letter. I am sorry my letter conveyed the idea that I am depressed – I assure you I am not in the least, but quite well & happy. I was naturally a little down over the sad news from France, but as I said, it was only what I expected. I was only joking about my shoulder, too. Of course, as wounds go, it is only a scratch; but even a scratch takes time.

I met Fryer & his fiasco[1] this afternoon & we had tea at the Popular. Tomorrow I am meeting him alone & I dare say we shall go to the Coliseum. I have been to the Palladium a couple of times & to the revue at the Hippodrome,

---

[1] *Fryer & his fiasco*: i.e. fiancée; Bill Fryer served as a Lance Bombardier in the Royal Field Artillery.

which I thought very good. I want to see Bric a Brac & The Byng Boys,[1] but some of these rotten places only have matinees on awkward days.

I hope you don't really mean I have spoilt Izaak for you. I wasn't running him down. The things I have pointed out only help to make the book interesting. If he had known as much as we do now the book would be unreadable. I dare say you would like to know what I am reading now. I have finished the sketches by Bret Harte & admired them very much. Then I read "Hushed Up" by Wm Le Queux & felt nauseated. This afternoon I got "The Blue Bird" by Maeterlinck & "The Antagonists" by E. Temple Thurstow. Do you know the latter's "City of Beautiful Nonsense"? It is rather a sweet tale.

Sorry the Thermos idea doesn't work. The alternative seems to be a spirit lamp & small kettle. Why not try a Tommy's Cooker?

I hear that Aunt Lyd is in a bad way. It seems that she is practically out of her mind. With Vernon's wife in much the same case, the Dormor's seem to be having their share of misfortune.

Please give my love to dad & tell him that it is the invariable habit when parcels come to men who have left the Batt[n] to share them out among his section. As I have participated in many such myself I am very willing that others should now have mine. I doubt if the postal people would return them, anyway. Letters are returned if possible. So far as I can make out there are five left of the Platoon as it trained in England, but the draft men we had out from time to time were luckier.

My shoulder is rather painful to-day & is discharging again, so you won't see me this week, anyway.

Please thank Neville for his note. I will drop him a line one of these days.

Much love to all,

Yrs affectionately

Roland

~

---

[1] *Bric a Brac & The Byng Boys*: like many soldiers home on leave or convalescing, Roland took in the shows at the London theatres. 'The Bing (sic) Boys Are Here' was the first of in a series of highly popular 'Bing Boys' revues which played at the Alhambra Theatre in London in the last two years of the war. (Opening in April 1916 and starring George Robey and Violet Lorraine, the first revue popularised the song "If you were the only girl in the world, And I were the only boy").

[No. 44 – further information on his wound – recent reading – visit from father of missing soldier]

Ward H4
15/8/16

Dear Mother,

Many thanks for your letter. I haven't received the one you sent to France – doubt if I shall now. I have heard that the parcels got there.

The sketches of Bret Harte's did not contain any of those you mention. There were "Houses I have moved from" & various short humorous sketches. I don't quite understand you when you say you have got a book out of the library "for me". How long do they allow you to keep books out? I hope you are not serious when you say you are hoping to see me this week. I shan't get out until my wound is perfectly healed & well; which will not be this week. It is progressing satisfactorily. Perhaps I didn't tell you sufficient about it. The bullet travelled under the surface for some five inches, & possibly turned a little on emerging, for there is a wound about the length & breadth of your first two fingers, & of fair depth. This will naturally take some little time to heal completely.

Funnily enough, in a book I have just read, "Sir John Constantine" by Q, three old boys who meet periodically to drink & talk & so forth, are in the habit on those occasions of reading a passage from Isaak Walton, and at the one meeting recorded in the book they have just got to "the marrow of the thigh bone of a heron" when various things happen. I have read "Hetty Wesley" by the same author, & have now got "Buried Alive" by Arnold Bennett. This sounds funny, but you know what I mean. I have also read "The Picture of Dorian Gray" by Oscar Wilde. It is rather weird. He was a great genius I believe, but I have read none of his "Belle Lettres" – must get a volume or two I think. The thing I have read is simply a clever novel.

I met the man from my office who was in the 13th Fus^{rs}, & wounded in Jan^{ry}, last Saturday. He has just been transferred to a London Hospital. We went to see "The Byng Boys". It is awfully funny; but not so pretty as the Hippodrome Revue.

The father of one of the men in my section who was killed came to see me yesterday, but unfortunately I was out. He is coming again. I have written to the people of one or two others. The official report, as I expected, is "missing, believed killed" which is rather rotten for their people, who naturally are glad to hear anything they can.

I haven't any news. Have you heard from Dormor lately? The weather here has temporarily broken up. Hope you are all well. Best love to all,

Yours affectionately

Roland

~

[No. 45 – death of Pickering confirmed – how time is spent in and out of hospital – a Zeppelin raid]

Ward G2.
Mile End Mily Hosp[1].
Bancroft Rd E
28/8/16

Dear Mother,

Many thanks for your letter, & please also thank Gwyneth for hers. Will you note that I am now in a different ward.

I had a visit from Mrs Hill[1] yesterday. It seems that Mrs Pickering has been writing to her to try & find out my address, but all Mrs Hill could give her was my address at Coventry. So if you hear anything you needn't bother about it, as I have already written to Mrs Pickering. Pickering died of a bad spine wound, & was buried with military honours at Abbeville on July 19th – the day I arrived England.

I can't think of much news for you to-day. I haven't got the Sketch Book yet but possibly may do to-day. I haven't had much time while I have been out lately.

On Friday I went & spent an hour or two at Vin's, who started his holidays in the middle of the week. He & Charlie are going to Brighton on Monday. They won't have much of a time if the weather doesn't improve. It's rather beastly here.

I am getting a trifle fed up with being in hospital. The days we can't get out are distinctly boring. Still, to leave here means to go back to France I suppose, which is out of the frying pan into the fire. The end of the war seems to be the only thing worth looking forward to.

On Saturday afternoon I went down to Herne Hill with a fellow from the office. He has a very decent house down there, & a nice wife. We played billiards on a small table. Unfortunately the hours we are allowed out make visits of that kind so very short. One or two others have asked me to go, but mostly they live so far away as to make it not worth while going at all.

We had a Zeppelin raid the other night, as you know. I heard the guns firing, but not very near. They dropped a bomb on the Greenwich Power Station, & the whole L. B. & S. C. Ry[2] electric service was suspended when I went down to Vin's on Friday. Everybody was under the impression they had been frightened away from London; but as it turns out they don't seem to have much to be frightened of.

The last man from the 10th went out last Friday, so I have outstayed them all. I haven't heard from France for some little time, so don't know what the Batt[n] is doing.

Will write again when I think of anything to write about. Best love to all

R.

---

[1] *Mrs Hill*: Roland's landlady from Leytonstone.
[2] *L. B. & S. C. Ry*: the London Borough and Southern Counties Railway.

[No. 46 – concerns about the health of relatives – recent reading]

P.S. Have you got used to letters only taking
a few hours on the way? It nearly always
gives me a shock when you refer to things
only mentioned a couple of days previously.

Ward G2
M.E. M. H[1]
Bancroft Rd E
31/8/16

Dear Dad,

Many thanks for your letter. From reading Aunt Nell's letter you will gather about as much about Aunt Lyd as I know myself. Her malady seems to be acute depression or melancholia so far as I can make out, with suicidal tendencies. I don't know if Aunt Nell is right about Miss Smyth – Aunt Lyd always used to seem very glad to go there, & often wrote to say how she loved the country walks. Certainly she seemed to hold Miss Smyth a little in awe. You will find a detailed account of the lady & my impression of Aunt Lyd there in a letter to Gwyneth, which I was reading when I was home on leave. Neither do I know the facts of Auntie Annie's alleged refusal to have her at Melcombe. I know that Auntie Annie has often said to me – personally & in letters – that she wished Aunt Lyd would come to Oxford instead of going to Grimsby where she didn't have a very good time but thought it her duty to be to look after Aunt Nell.

Glad to hear Dormor is still well.

Will you please tell Mother if she wants me to read the "Sketch Book" she had better get it to me. The book-shop keepers of whom I have enquired for it so far have looked at me as though they thought I was probably suffering from shell-shock & said gently but firmly that they haven't got it. At present I have the Novel Magazine, "Black Beauty" with a note on the cover that it is the hundred millionth copy or the thousand millionth edition or something, & "Queen Mary" by "Mr" Tennyson, of which I purchased a 1st Edition for 2/-, incurring a complete waste of 1/6.

On Monday I saw Razzle Dazzle at the Empire – not bad – but I'm getting blasé now so far as revues are concerned.

Have you seen the Big Push films?[1] Best Love.

R.

~

---

[1] *The Big Push films*: the official film of The Battle of the Somme; films because its length meant it ran to several reels. Much of the film dealt with the preparations for the offensive and it was released before the battle had run its course – Roland's reference being dated August 31st.

[No. 47 – passing time in London – 'a lovely Zepp raid']

Beastly cold to-day & dull. A brother of Pickering's came to see me, Sunday. Not a bad fellow & rather like Pick. Said his wife & a girl friend stopping with them wanted to come, so I told him to send them along on Wednesday. Wonder what I've let myself in for.

> Best love to all
>
> R

Ward G2
Mile End
Military Hosp[1]
Bancroft Rd E
5/9/16

Have just read "The Guilty River" by Wilkie Collins. I wonder where I got hold of the impression that he could write.

Dear Mother,

Many thanks for your letter. I haven't got anything to tell you, so will just write a line to say that I am still here – haven't been strafed by Zepps or anything – and that I hope to be home before long.

I had one p.c. from Vin at Brighton; he was fairly cheerful but they must have had a rotten week. I saw Little Tich[1] at the Palladium on Saturday – first time for years. I think he is one of the best comedians going. He is quite as funny as any of the best-known stars, without relying, as most of them do, principally on vulgarity for his wit. Yesterday I went to see Mrs Lennol at 109 Gleneagle Rd. I had two glasses of whisky. I don't know if you realise the tragedy of my position. In the hospital uniform you can't get a drink anyhow except by the charity of people as above; & they are liable to a fine of a couple of hundred or so for giving it you. I haven't had half a dozen drinks in the last 3 months.

We had a lovely Zepp raid[2] the other night. The one that was brought down was distinctly seen to fall from the hospital, but our ward isn't in the right direction, so I didn't see it. I was watching one being fired at a little way away when I spotted another exactly overhead, & got the wind up. I don't think they dropped bombs anywhere near here but shrapnel from our guns fell in the grounds.

They have cut down our hours for going out to 2 till 6.30. They made it 2 – 6 first & raised such a storm they made it 2 – 7. Then the sisters groused they couldn't get their dressings done in the evening, so they compromised with 2 – 6.30.

∼

---

[1] *Little Tich*: Harry Ralph (1867-1928), a popular English music hall comedian, whose most famous routine was the Big Boot Dance.

[2] *a lovely Zepp raid*: the raid by 16 German airships on the night of September 2nd / 3rd, 1916, which resulted in the destruction north of Enfield of Airship SL11, shot down by Lieutenant William L. Robinson, who became the first pilot to shoot down an airship over Britain. The event was witnessed by thousands of Londoners and resulted in the award of the VC to Robinson.

[No. 48 – recent reading – an 'outing' and other visits – on getting thin on top]

> Ward G2
> Mile End Mily Hosp[1]
> Bancroft Rd E
> 14/9/16

Dear Mother,

Many thanks for your letter enclosing the Sketch Book; one or two chapters of which I have already read. I won't express any opinion about them until I have seen them all. I am in the middle of De Quincey's "Confessions of an Opium Eater", & being, as I say, in the middle, don't seem to be getting any nearer the opium part of the business. I must confess I wish he would get on with it, as he is apt to be tedious. I have also got the Professor at the Breakfast Table, who has not the same charm as the Autocrat; & five more short pieces of Balzac's.

I had a very good "outing" yesterday afternoon – the first I have been to. Fifteen of us were taken by some awfully nice people in four private cars to Richmond, where we had tea at the Castle Hotel. Being a Wednesday it was especially pleasant.

Am looking forward to seeing Gwyneth over the week end. Now that the time is drawing near for me to leave London, the number of things I still want to do is appalling. I have just heard that a friend of mine in 9 Platoon is at the Sth African Hospital, Richmond. He is a Sol[r], & as he gets out everyday, he has taken his old rooms in Dover St Piccadilly. I spent Tuesday afternoon with him there, & am having lunch with him at his club to-morrow. I am anxious to see the Somme Pictures, but don't seem to have a minute to spare.

I reached an epoch in my life the day before yesterday. A barber told me I was "getting rather thin on the top, Sir". Somebody or other painted a picture of a woman finding the first grey hair. Surely a man being told for the first time he is getting thin on top is worthy of similar commemoration. Of course he wanted me to buy a bottle of lotion of some sort & of course I refused to do any sort of favour to a person who had so insulted me – to call attention to any personal imperfections is an insult, & I don't see why barbers should have any particular license in this respect – but I believe the blighter was to some extent right.

Must write a note to Gwyneth. Hope to see you all before long now. Best love from

> Yours affecly
>
> Roland

P.S. I quite understand about nobody coming up here to see me. I didn't expect you to in the least, as there was absolutely no necessity for it. I don't remember telling you my wound was a bad one – all I said was that it wasn't going to heal so quickly as you seemed to think.

I thought the article on garden pests very funny.

~

Chapter 6

DOVER, OCTOBER 1916 – FEBRUARY 1917
LETTERS 49-58

Letters 49 – 58 refer to the period following Roland's discharge from hospital. After a period of leave, he was ordered to join the 6th Royal Fusiliers – a reserve battalion – at Dover. He remained with them until December 1916 when he was transferred to the 32nd Training Reserve Battalion, also in Dover, as his medical category had been reassessed. For the most part, these were dull and monotonous days, with "one decent hotel" and the occasional weekend pass providing some scant consolation. However, he found companions amongst other soldiers in the reserve battalions.

In January, he learnt of the death of another close friend from the pre-war days, Bill Morris. He was also depressed at the prospect of having to make a full return to Army life, "which after two years I still loathe with all the hatred of which I am capable". It was largely to delay going back that he reluctantly decided to apply for a commission. However, he received orders to join a draft for East Africa before his papers came through and the issue was not raised again in his letters.

~

[No. 49 – the move to Dover – first impressions of new quarters and occupants – initial thoughts about applying for a commission]

> No. 5 Company
> 6th Bat. R. F. Regt
> Duke of York's Schools,
> Dover
> 13/10/1916

Dear Dad,

I arrived here safely last night, & at present have seen too little of my surroundings to be able to express much of an opinion about them. I didn't see anything of Vinnie in London, either at Euston at 4.30 or the alternative I suggested in the Strand at 5.15, which rather annoyed me; though the explanation is probably that he didn't get my card in time. I caught the 6.22 at Cannon St & got into Dover about 9. I then had nearly 3 miles to walk, this place being in an isolated position some distance beyond the castle along the shore. There has been a thick sea fog with a drizzle all day to-day, though I should think it's pretty healthy. Our quarters are not bad. I can't make out quite what this has been in peace times; but it is a collection of groups of recently erected small houses covering an area of many acres. So far as quarters are concerned, therefore, it is not unlike being back in Assaye Married Quarters.[1] No. 5 Company is the one where gradual training is commenced, so apparently for 3 weeks I don't have much to do. If you are then medically fit you are posted to one of the Training Coys (1 – 4) & in due course (after six days leave) go out with a draft. If however the Training Coys are at full strength, large parties are sent to other Battns. A very large draft went only 3 days ago to St Albans, & this, I am told, included nearly the whole of the representatives of the 10th. My luck is out sometimes you see. I have only seen one man I knew slightly so far. He was wounded on the same day as I, & we came down the trenches together, through the gas &c but he couldn't walk very well, being wounded in the back, & stayed at the first dressing station, while I went on to Albert. The men in the same house as I are a nondescript lot, & I don't anticipate making any life-long friendships. Men are constantly rejoining, however, & someone I know may turn up in time. I believe the next crowd to go from here will go to St Margarets Bay, which is a hole, & I hope it won't include me.

I am told that many of the old 10th are getting commissions now, & it is very possible that by worrying in the right quarters I might do so too. I am quite unable to make up my mind on the point though. It seems to me that the only reason one can urge for really wanting a commission is to have a better time – to get out of a good deal of work, & live a more comfortable sort of life: and that seems to me rather a poor thing; especially when it is only a matter of a year or two, & not of a permanent career. I must think it over seriously. If I try to get one I am told that the simplest way is for you to apply to the War Office for my papers, & having got these I can approach the people here.

When I know a bit more about the place I will write again. Best love to all.

Roland

~

[No. 50 – convalescent life – decision to apply for a commission – hatred of Army life]

No 771 L/Cpl RDM
No. 5 Coy
6th R F
Duke of Yorks School
Dover
22/10/16

Dear Mother,

Although I have now been here a week I haven't a great deal to add to my last letter. I don't have a great deal to do & can't really grumble at my present circumstances, though what the difference will be when my three weeks of convalescence are up remains to be seen. Our daily programme of parades is a short walk, usually about half a mile each way, at 7, 10 & 2. There are fatigues of

---

[1] *Assaye Married Quarters*: accommodation at the Assaye Barracks, in which the 10th Royal Fusiliers had stayed in October 1914; named after the Battle of Assaye, 1803, in India.

course, but up to now my stripe has preserved me from anything in the least arduous. For the last two days I have been on an escort of prisoners being tried by court-martial at Dover Castle. Do you know anything about this Castle? It's rather an imposing looking place, rather like the Tower of London, as to appearance, but more resembling Dinas Bran in situation[1].

I usually spend my evenings in town, despite the distance, & the tremendous climb back. There is one decent cinema & a hippodrome, & several not bad places of refreshment.

The grub here is good – the best I have had in the Army, I think; & we eat it sitting at a table off plates which I don't wash up. The house is cheerless, & there is always a bitter wind up here on the cliffs; but I've no doubt it's very healthy. I can conscientiously say that the appetite I had for all my meals put together while on leave would not amount to that which I bring to any single meal here, & I didn't feel a tenth so comfortable in the luxurious bed I always got at Oxford as wrapped up in my three blankets here. I don't know whether this proves that the worst situation has its compensations or that the best one has its drawbacks, but it certainly shows the cussedness of things.

As soon as I am marked fit & passed into a training Company I intend to make every endeavour to get a commission. I don't know if the decision is a wise one, or a creditable one; but I can't resist the temptation to try. As likely as not I may not be successful, & then I shall be able to resign myself better to going without.

The weather on the whole has been good. It is marvellous how clearly France can be seen across the Straits. I had no idea you could do more than just descry it; but on a clear day it looks as though you could swim across. The country inland is perfectly visible for some distance, & it is difficult to believe it really is France.

I hope you are still feeling the better for our trip to Llangollen. I have often thought of the Christmas Pantomime Fairy Glen & the spring from which we drank en route for the Worlds End. Next time we must make a point of actually reaching the Elizabethan house.

I have since wondered if you really had as good a time there as you might have done. I am afraid you must have found my society a trifle dull. I realised at the time that I wasn't being exactly brilliant, but didn't seem to be able to help it. I think it was due in a large measure to the sub-conscious oppression of the knowledge of my imminent return to Army life, which after two years I still loathe with all the hatred of which I am capable. We must have another holiday after the war, when the horizon is all clear.

I hope all are well at home. With best love to all from

Yrs affectionately

Roland

P. S. Have heard from Vin. He didn't get my p.c. till the evening.

---

[1] *resembling Dinas Bran in situation*: the site of a ruined castle high above the River Dee near Llangollen.

[No. 51 – problems with the post – the locality and church services – gales]

> No 771 L/Cpl RDM
> No 5 Coy, 6th R. F.
> Morley House
> St Margarets at Cliffe
> Nr Dover.
> 7/11/16

Dear Mother,

I was very sorry to hear yesterday that you are having such an anxious time. I am afraid your second letter to me has miscarried, for the letters I got last night were the only ones I have received from home since your first one which crossed mine. The post in this Batt[n] is very slack. Sometimes my letters are brought to me, sometimes they hang about in the Corporals mess until I happen to find them. Then letters are pinched in the hope of finding money, & so on. I'm sorry this one should have gone astray.

Shall be glad to hear how Phil gets on. You don't say how Geoff was looking after his experiences.[1]

We are still at this village, & I am still in the dark as to our future. At present it suits me pretty well, so far as anything in the Army can. I don't get much exercise from the Army, but contrive to put a little in on my own. There is one decent hotel on the cliff, the Granville. I had dinner there the other night. The bill was 12/6 for two, so you can see the vintage was not "old brown".

The village boasts a rather fine Norman Church. I went to Matins there last Sunday & was very disappointed. Hoping to hear a simple service, with a village choir singing in dialect, & a plain expounding of the scriptures by a kindly old parson, you can imagine I was pretty sorry to have to listen to the Litany, fully intoned, & the Communion Service with the Nicene Creed sung by half a dozen ladies & a few old gentlemen as choir, accompanied by an organ with about the range of a good harmonium, & to have to go into abstruse questions of public morality & the labour problem as affected by the National Mission.

I am hoping to spend this week end in London. I have a pass in, but several things may conspire to stop it. I am looking forward to going up very much.

We have had enormous gales here. The boats anchored in the Deal Roads, which make quite a picture from the cliffs, had a very rough time. Strenuous efforts are being made to refloat the Destroyer aground here, but so far unsuccessfully. The whole of the fore part is detached & lying some 200 yds away, where she first struck the rocks.

Please thank Gwyneth & Hilda for their letters. I will write to Gwyneth before long I daresay.

> Yours affectionately
> Roland

---

[1] *Geoff's experiences*: Roland's half-brother, Geoffrey, enlisted in the Army in July 1916 at the age of 18 years. By the time of his discharge in March 1920, he had served as a Private with the Essex Regiment, the Royal Fusiliers, the Royal West Kents and the Suffolk Regiment.

[No. 52 – Gray's Elegy – medical inspection – a weekend in London]

No 771 L/Cpl RDM
No 5 Coy, 6 R. F.
Morley House
St Margarets at Cliffe
Nr Dover.
17/11/16

Dear Mother,

You will be glad to hear I have received your letter safely this time. I am sorry about the last one but I'm afraid it wasn't my fault.

Glad to hear the news of Phil, Geoff &c. Do you mean to say that the whole business about Phillip[1] is over, after having gone so far? Surely something can be done about it.

I was positively amazed at your asking me about that quotation. Why didn't you ask Neville? The lines – & the context is equally fine –

> "Full many a gem of purest ray serene
> "The dark unfathomed caves of ocean bear
> "Till many a flower (not rose) is born to blush unseen
> "And waste its sweetness on the desert air"

are from Gray's Elegy.

I am really not having half a bad time down here. I know a couple of very decent & interesting fellows; & have little to worry about & less to do. All the men in the same category as myself (A3) went up for medical inspections on Wednesday, & to my great delight I was not passed fit, but put back for a further period of A3, so I am safe for another week or two here. The fit men go back to the Schools to-morrow & start carrying a pack & rifle about with them. I can't do anything in the matter of my comm[n] until I am fit, unless I can get hold of the Army form of application & get it filled up in readiness.

I spent the week end in town, & had a pretty quiet time. On Friday evening I had a grooming at Victoria, did myself well at the Strand Corner House, & went down to Streatham. On Saty morning I went & saw a fellow I know in hospital at Fitzroy Square, & then to the office; after lunch billiards with the man aforesaid. Tea at the Maison Riche, & at 6.30 met a fellow from the office; more billiards & the second house at the Palladium. Sunday nothing.

[Rest of letter missing]

~

---

[1] *the whole business about Phillip*: Phillip Mountfort, one of Roland's half-brothers, and twin of Neville, was born handicapped and had to be cared for throughout his life but was a much-loved member of the family.

[No. 53 – the move to Longhill – continued A3 classification – Canterbury Cathedral]

> 771 L/Cpl RDM
> E Coy. Hut No 15
> 32nd Training Reserve
> Longhill Camp
> Dover.
> Tuesday **[November 28th]**

Dear Mother,

I don't know whether I wrote to you last, or you to me; but I fancy I owe you a letter. You see we have left St Margarets. It was a most awful blow: I'm afraid I shall never strike a place like it in the Army again. I was getting to know an awful lot of people in the place, & nice people too. We had any amount of invitations to tea, & I could have chosen between at least three places at which to spend Xmas, if, as we sincerely hoped, we had been there. Last Saturday we heard we were moving on Sunday; & accordingly in the afternoon all the A3 men were taken back to the Duke of Yorks, from which on Monday we were transferred here, about 1 mile away & nearer Dover. What they are going to do with us now goodness only knows; they brought the weirdest mixture, about 200 men, some fit, some half fit & some hopeless cripples.

I was marked A3 again because my wound was adjudged insufficiently healed. They didn't examine hearts & lungs. I daresay I shall get another med. exam here.

Until I get some idea of what they are going to do with us I haven't much to tell you. I daresay we might be pretty comfortable here if they'll give us half a chance. From what it says in the papers to-day it doesn't look as though there will be any Xmas leave.[1]

I went into Canterbury the other week, but didn't have time to do much beyond glancing at the Cathedral. There was evensong at 3.15 which rather interfered with our view, so we went to the service. It is held in what I believe is called the Choir, which in this instance is quite shut off from the rest, ingress being obtained only through little doors here & there. It is rather a wonderful place, all velvet cushions & huge great tomes, with weird little stalls for all the canons & bishops & people. We sat absolutely mixed up with the Choir in the funniest way. There were a few big pots there, with long beards & bowed heads, looking like the prophets of old; who were escorted to their stalls, & shut up, & curtains drawn round them; rather like a Court of Justice. The singing was nothing out of the way, only half the Choir being in action, the others apparently saving their energy for Sunday's effort. I rather enjoyed the service; but my companion, an out-&-out High Churchman, with matured views on such matters, didn't think much of it.

---

[1] *Xmas leave*: presumably a reference to the Board of Trade's call for a decrease in 'unnecessary travel' on the railways.

Sorry to hear Phillip's case has fallen through. Please tell Gwyneth I'm very sorry I haven't written to her yet. I meant to have done this weekend from Morley House, but this beastly move is so unsettling.

Hope you are all well. I have had a beastly cold & a good deal of neuralgia.

Best love to all from

Yours affectionately

Roland

~

[No. 54 – continued A3 classification]

What do you think of the leave reg[ns]?[1] I like the wording of them. "Munition workers holidays will be <u>restricted</u> & soldiers will be asked to <u>give up</u> their week end leave."

771 L/Cpl RDM
E Coy No 15 Hut
32nd Training Reserve
Longhill Camp
Dover
6/12/16

Dear Mother,

I thought I had better write & tell you that I rec[d] your letter & Gwyneth's this morning; also the previous one you refer to. So as you feared our letters have crossed, but it didn't make much difference. My category is still A3, but A3's seem to be rather differently treated here. We do about 5 hours a day, & play about with a rifle, though I don't think we have any equipment.

I don't know the author you mention. With reference to De Quincey it is undoubtedly his own life that he records in the "O. E."[2]. For the last few days I have been regretting that his cure for neuralgia cannot easily be used nowadays.

Will write again soon. Best love

R.

~

---

[1] *The leave reg[ns]*: in order to ease pressure on the railway system, the government announced travel restrictions on December 4th, 1916, which included a request to soldiers stationed at home to give up their weekend and Christmas leave. Soldiers on leave from the front were not affected.
[2] *"O.E."*: Opium Eater.

[No. 55 – the pros and cons of applying for a commission – Christmas 1916 – monotony of Army life]

> 771 L/Cpl RDM
> E Coy No 10 (N.B.) Hut
> 32nd Training Reserve
> Longhill Camp
> Dover
> 28/12/16

Dear Dad,

I have received my papers & am most obliged for the celerity with which you got them completed. I am sorry that you are rather perturbed at the idea of my getting a comm[n], but as I pointed out, the thing is by no means a fait accompli, & the putting in of these papers is only the first step in a long process which has in its course a thousand & one further chances of turning out unsuccessfully. By far the most likely thing is that I shall be sent out with a draft (perhaps to Salonica) before the business matures, & then the W.O. have a happy knack of losing your papers, & you don't get recalled. If no hitch occurs, in four or five weeks time I should be posted to a cadet school for a date three or 4 weeks after that. That brings us to about the end of Feb. Then I get 4 months at the School – end of June, & then at least 4 weeks in England – end of July. So the prospect is either to go in the middle of Jan. in the ranks or at the end of July as a Sub. Why the war may be over. Then officers are occasionally wounded & not killed you know. And anyway <u>somebody</u> has got to be officers even if they do get killed.

If we get sent back to the Duke of Yorks they will probably want a new set of papers for the benefit of the Col. of the 6th. If that happens I will reconsider the matter seriously before worrying you again.

I am sorry your Xmas was "funny". Mine wasn't much like a Christmas. There was no real "goodwill" about the Coy dinner we had here, (a minimum of turkey & plum pudding; watery beer & no fruit) & the 10th R.F. dinner at the Lord Warden, though extremely nice up to a certain point, cost us a pretty penny, & finished up quite early & rather disastrously with 2 or 3 men under the table & one subsequently in the hands of the military police. On Boxing Day we did a full days drill, finishing at 4.30; a most infamous thing, as time immemorial has given us a right to a half day off.

I have had little correspondence; one Christmas card, &. from Hilda Simmonds, a photo in lieu thereof which, entre nous, is one of the poorest specimens of portraiture I have ever encountered.

The days here are horribly dull & monotonous; & we live solely for the evening. Am afraid it costs a good deal of money, as I have a good supper practically every night; but I read my pocket Omar & reconcile conscience & reason.

Please thank all the children for their nice letters. I am pretty fit in health – in fact so far as I can judge, of my appearance I have never looked better. The Army is splendid no doubt for the "in corpore sano" but for the "mens sana" it is a wash out. Wm Le Queux & the Daily Mirror are about my mark these days.

I am mistrustful of all this peace talk.[1] A lot of people are optimistic in the belief that the Allies' attitude is bluff; but I'm not inclined to take a bright view of the situation as yet.

Best love to all from

Your affectionate son

Roland

~

[No. 56 – prospect of leave – progress of application for commission – death of Morris]

> 771 L/Cpl RDM
> E Coy No 10 Hut
> 32nd Training Reserve
> Longhill Camp
> Dover
> 4/1/17

Dear Mother,

Many thanks for your letter.

After your last disappointment I rather hesitate to mention it, but at present I am supposed to be having 4 days leave starting next Saturday. This is final leave, & after it I shall be liable for an expeditionary draft at any moment. All sorts of things may happen of course. The principal thing is that my papers have passed the Colonel here & have gone to the Brigade office; consequently just as I am leaving on Saturday I shall be told I have to see the Brigadier at 9 a.m. on Monday or something of that sort; or I may get home & get recalled by wire. So you will make no sort of preparation. I shall leave here pretty early on Sat. I hope, & will let you know by wire from London, & then if there's time you can get some sausages for supper, or some luxury like that.

Yesterday I received the bitterest shock of the war, except perhaps that of the death of Pickering. Morris has died of wounds.[2] So my two oldest & best friends of pre-war days are gone. If this goes on much longer civil life will be a poor thing to come back to after all. The office won't be the same place now. In all the years I knew him we never had a single difference, & of my life in London he is associated with practically every pleasant recollection.

Best love to all

R

---

[1] *all this peace talk*: on December 12th, 1916, Germany had issued a Peace Note suggesting a compromise peace. Six days later, President Wilson of the U.S.A. sent his own Peace Note to the belligerents. On December 26th, in reply to Wilson's Note, the Germans suggested a peace conference. However, these initiatives came to nothing when the Entente refused to discuss peace without a German commitment to reparations.

[2] *Morris has died of wounds*: Gunner 137060 William Charles Morris of the 12th Siege Battery, Royal Garrison Artillery, died on December 20th, 1916, aged 27 years. He had been wounded in the abdomen on November 19th and lingered more than a month before succumbing to his wounds. He died at XI Stationary Hospital in Rouen and is buried in the town's St Sever Cemetery.

[No. 57 – preparations for departure]

Dover

9/2/17

Dear Mother,

The latest rumour, & I shouldn't be surprised if it's a true one is that we are leaving tomorrow (Saty) at 7 p.m. This is a beastly nuisance, as I was looking forward to a decent farewell evening to-morrow. However, it can't be helped.

I am sending home a few trifles I don't want to throw away but which it isn't worth while taking with me. They include the 10 which I wore on my collar in France, the stripes off the tunic in which I was wounded; & the identification disk I wore round my neck the whole time. After a year of toil I'm afraid it is a little grimy, & my distressing little friends used to use it as a tight rope, but I don't think you need to be afraid of it now.

I have written to the Prudtl telling them I am going out; if they reply you can open the letter, & needn't forward it unless it is anything important.

Please tell <u>Dad</u> if he doesn't receive my insce Pol. from someone in the Dept, the S.W. Branch can give all particulars of it if occasion should arise.

Very busy to-day with one thing and another. It's a bit of an upheaval.

Best love.

R

Will try & drop another p.c. or write to-morrow

~

[No. 58 – Post card addressed to:-]

J. Mountfort Esq, Grinshill, 43 Park Rd, Coventry.   10/2/17

Your letter & Mother's just arrived to-night. We leave at 7.30 p.m. & it is nearly 6 now, so no time to write much.

Goodbye & dear love to you all.

R.

~

Chapter 7

AT SEA AND IN SOUTH AFRICA,
FEBRUARY – JUNE 1917
LETTERS 59-65

In February 1917, Roland joined a draft for East Africa, landing in Cape Town in March. Here he was posted to the 25th (Service) Battalion, Royal Fusiliers (Frontiersmen), who were doing garrison duties whilst being brought back up to strength.

The 25th Battalion of the Royal Fusiliers was one of the most unusual and colourful battalions to serve in the Great War – the history of the Royal Fusiliers describes the Battalion as "a romantic body of adventurers". In February 1915, Colonel Daniel Driscoll, D.S.O., who had led 'Driscoll's Scouts' in the Boer War, was given permission to raise an infantry battalion for service in East Africa. About a third of its members came from the 'Legion of Frontiersmen', an organisation established by Roger Pocock in 1904-05, in the aftermath of the Boer War. An adventurer and author, Pocock had appealed for men with "experience of action abroad to come together for comradeship and service to the State in time of need". By 1914, there were more than 10,000 Frontiersmen, drawn from all walks of life and scattered throughout the Empire. Many enlisted in other units in the early months of the war but sufficient were drawn to the 25th Royal Fusiliers for the Battalion to merit the title "Frontiersmen".

Roland described the original 25th as "a tough lot ... They came from everywhere under the sun". They included the famous big game hunter and explorer, Frank Selous, who was already 64 years old in 1915 and one of the oldest soldiers in the British Army. (He was mortally wounded in a fire-fight in January 1917). Reputedly, the Battalion also contained naturalists, American cowboys, veterans of the French Foreign Legion, a former Honduran general, a lighthouse keeper, music hall comedians, university professors, a lion tamer and a member of a vaudeville team who could climb stairs on his head! In East Africa the Fusiliers became known as "the old and the bold" – or, less flatteringly, the "Boozaliers". So great was their expertise presumed to be that the Battalion was sent on active service without preliminary training – the only unit in the British Army to be so treated. In fact, many of its members had never fired a rifle. Nonetheless, having reached Mombasa in May 1915, they were in action by June.

The 25th Battalion of the Royal Fusiliers became part of a campaign that had been waged since 1914 to take control of German East Africa. The Fusiliers found themselves pitted against a determined and resourceful enemy. Colonel von Lettow-Vorbeck, with 10,000 German troops supported by native auxiliaries, proved to be a master of guerrilla warfare who would successfully defy Allied forces, many times greater in strength, for the duration of the war. However, it was not merely the enemy that took its toll but also the climate and conditions in which men served. Diseases included malaria (and its even more dangerous complication, blackwater fever), dysentery and typhoid, and troops were also assailed by various parasites. Medical provision was patchy and the ratio in the British forces of non-battle casualties to battle casualties reached more than 30 to 1 during 1916. As one member of the 25*th* Royal Fusiliers put it, "I wish to hell I was in France! There one lives like a gentleman and dies like a man. Here one lives like a pig and dies like a dog."[1]

By Christmas of 1916, only 60 of the original 1,166 members of the 25*th* Royal Fusiliers were still in the field. In February, the Battalion was temporarily withdrawn from the campaign and sent to Cape Town for three months rest. It was here that Roland joined his new comrades.

~

[No. 59 (No date – but March 1917) – the voyage to South Africa – adjusting to the heat – inoculations – books – pilfering on board ship]

At Sea.

Dear Dad,

Many happy returns from you all, I've no doubt. I don't suppose you have my last letter yet, as it didn't go for more than a week after I wrote it. We reached a port[2] on the **[word censored]** after having been just a fortnight out of sight of land. There we remained three days. Arrangements had been made for the Fus[rs]. to go ashore for a route march on the second day, but it was cancelled at the last moment, & on the third day we sailed. I was most disappointed not to see more of the place than could be discerned from the boat – that is to say a collection of white houses with

[next 11 lines censored]

The only unusual excitement during these three days was derived from the niggers who came out in fragile canoes, to sell fruit, dive for pennies & collect fragments of meat & bread.

We have been at sea again for about a week. Our attire now is distinctly picturesque. It consists of a pair of trousers rolled above the knee, a shirt or vest, open at the throat with sleeves rolled to the elbow, a sun-helmet & an identity disc. It is really very comfortable & convenient. As one man said, when you get up in the morning you pull on half a pair of trousers & you are dressed up ready to go to church. A confirmed pessimist would call attention to the necessity of regularly including arms, legs, feet & chest in the daily ablutions, but I doubt if from choice he would put his boots on again. The weather is not so enormously hot, though it is only a few days since we crossed the line. It must be remembered however, that at sea there is always a breeze, & one need never stand in the sun. The unprotected parts of the deck are painful to the bare feet at mid-day.

---

[1] Unnamed soldier quoted in 'The Great War in East Africa' by Byron Farwell, W. W. Norton & Company, 1986.
[2] *We reached a port*: presumably Freetown in Sierra Leone – see the start of Letter 60.

We have been inoculated (with two injections) against cholera; this time on the chest. I suppose there isn't an available site remaining on our arms. It is comforting to know I am now presumably immune from cholera, tetanus, typhoid & small-pox. If only I were similarly sure about tooth-ache, indigestion & liver!

I wish to goodness I had a few decent books. I took a couple with me & they have issued a hundred sevenpenny editions for circulation on board – mostly piffle of Le Queux's &c, which you read in an hour & a half, kick yourself for so much wasted time, & hawk round for 3 or 4 days trying to swap for some more bilge of the same sort. Most of my time is spent playing auction bridge but since there is nothing else to do I'm getting fed up with it. With a little decent literature to vary the recreation I should be moderately happy.

The weather is good now, but we ran into violent thunderstorms a few days ago. What a dream of delight this voyage would be in civilian life. With comfortable quarters, good grub, decent people, a drop of whisky when you felt like it, & the freedom of action which after all this time I am almost beginning to regard as something very delightful, but wholly mythical & unreal, this experience would be enjoyable beyond words. It is an undoubted fact that I have never yet earnestly longed for anything, but sooner or later I have had my wish, yet always under such changed conditions, in such altered circumstances, & with such restrictions & penalties that it has been barely worth the having. So here.

The amount of pilfering that goes on aboard this ship is appalling. It was well for the renowned Ben Adhem[1] that he was more charitably minded than I am, or I'm afraid he would have said "Write me as one that loves his fellow gentlemen", making it a matter of some uncertainty whether his name would have occupied that same prominent position in the angelic roll-book we are told that on the next night it actually did. I thank the saints that my army training & my year in France were spent with the Battalion they were and not with the Battalion they might have been. If the hardships had not been mitigated by the society of real good fellows, many of whom I am glad to think will be my friends in after life – "though some are fallen asleep" – I honestly don't know if I could have endured them, though I suppose I could. To return, however. The system is this. A man loses an article somehow – that is to say he becomes "deficient" of it, either by dropping it down a drain, or selling it for Woodbines, or just mislaying it. Very well. The next day he is no longer deficient, but by a strange coincidence, a perfect stranger in another mess or another deck or even another regiment finds that his personal property is lacking a precisely similar article. So now the ball is rolling & it rolls about the ship until it enters a cul de sac represented by an unfortunate whose education, though possibly of wider scope than his fellows in many directions, regrettably has not included the science of petty theft. So it stops; but there are plenty of others to take its' place & the games go merrily on.

We have seen a few flying fish though not a lot. From a short distance they resemble swallows more than anything, skimming over the waves for varying distances up to 20 yards & then tumbling in again.

---

[1] *Ben Adhem*: 'Abou ben Adhem' – the poem by Leigh Hunt. Abou's love of his fellow men meant that his name led the list of those "whom love of God had blessed".

I doubt if this will start homeward for a week or so; but you'll get it some old time, I hope.

Best love to all from

Your affectionate son

Roland

P.S. I heard from the office just before I left, & I have my usual annual increment.[1]

R

P.P.S. I wonder what is happening in the world. It will soon be a month since I saw a paper, though we get scraps of war news by wireless.   R

~

[No. 60 – arrival at Cape Town – joining the 25th Battalion – impressions of Cape Town – dinner at the 'Grand' – stripe given up – the convoy out – meals – Murzenberg]

17th March 1917

Dear Mother,

I can at last give you a little more news about what is happening.

After we left Sierra Leone – our first stopping place – nothing occurred of any importance until we reached Cape Town last Tuesday *[March 13th]*. Here the Fusiliers were suddenly ordered to disembark & a few hours later we trod terra firma for the first time for a month. We marched to the station & came down about 7 miles by train to a place called Wynberg, where we are at present stationed. The explanation is this – the 25th Battalion to which we were to be drafted, after having been in German East for nearly two years, has come here for a rest. They arrived the day following, & we are now handed over to them & posted to various Companies. They expect to be here about six weeks, their subsequent movements being uncertain. The chances seem to be they will either go back to German East or to Mesopotamia.

This seems to be a very pleasant spot. Although it is – I believe – their autumn, the weather is pretty sultry. Up to the present there is not much doing, & yesterday I went into Cape Town. There is nothing very extraordinary about it, & yesterday it was duller than ever owing to the presence of the Australians in the town, which is the signal for every bar of any sort or description to close down entirely until their departure. We had dinner at the Grand Hotel, & the waiter solemnly asked whether we would take ginger ale or lemonade! It was a mysterious affair, that dinner. The price of food here seems to run about $1/3$ higher than at home, on the average, & the Grand being one of the best hotels in the place I expected a decent sized bill. But will you believe me, after a six course

---

[1] *my usual annual increment*: see introduction to Chapter 2 for the supportive attitude of the Prudential Company towards those employees who were in the forces.

dinner & coffee we were presented with a bill for 7/- for two. I'm going there again to see if it works every time. A 3/6 table d'hôte of that description seems to be a good investment. After dinner we went to the Tivoli, & saw a couple of concert parties.

Except for the presence of the coloured people, there is not a lot to remind you you are not in England. In fact the next station up from here – there are about eight between here & Cape Town; it reminds me of the Great Eastern more than anything – is called Kenilworth. Almost home from home, what?

On being posted to a Company in this Batt[n], among men who have been out here all this time & in a country about which I know nothing at all, I judged it best to give up my stripe, & my Company Officer somewhat reluctantly allowed me to do so. My address is now 47655 Pte R. D. M. No 14 Platoon D Coy, 25th R.F., E. African Expy Fce, G.P.O. London.

I gather from the papers that we don't seem to have missed much through not seeing one for a month. The Russian news[1] to-day is pretty startling though. By the time you get this I suppose you will know what it is all about. At present I can't make head or tail of it.

I hope you have my first letter by now. I believe it went to England from Sierra Leone on the same boat as Gen[l] Smuts.[2] Our boat was the Marathon, Aberdeen Line. There were six ships in the Convoy. Occasionally one came near enough for us to see the people on board, but usually we steamed in two lines of three at a distance of about a mile.

I am looking forward to getting a letter from you. My best wishes to Dad & Neville on their birthdays.

I may possibly add to this as I am not certain when the mail goes. If not, my best love to all.

Yours affectionately

Roland.

P.S. We have our meals in a weird order here. It amounts to tea, breakfast, dinner. At 8 a.m. we have tea, bread & butter & jam, at 1 p.m., coffee & bacon, & at 4.30 p.m. meat & vegetables. The idea is to avoid a big meal in the heat of the day, I suppose.   R.

P.P.S. Got a pass from 10 a.m. yesterday (Sunday) & went to Murzenberg, a sea side place about 6 miles down the line. Very small but quite nice. Surf bathing in the approved style. Sand is a dazzling white, giving the place a peculiar appearance after blighty. In the evening went into Cape Town. There is a magnificent pier there, brilliantly illuminated, or at least it seemed so after Dover.   R.

---

[1] *The Russian news*: popular uprisings in Russia in March 1917 (February by the contemporary Russian calendar), which led to the abdication of Tsar Nicholas II on March 15th, with power passing to the Provisional Government. The Bolsheviks did not seize power until November (October by the Russian calendar).

[2] *General Smuts*: the former Boer soldier and statesman who had been appointed in early 1916 to lead the British Imperial force in German East Africa; in March 1917 he was promoted to the British War Cabinet.

[No. 61 – life at Wynberg and Cape Town – enhanced status of ordinary British soldiers]

March
29th, 1917

Dear Mother,

This one sided letter writing is very unsatisfactory, but I suppose it can't be helped. The latest mail received here is dated some time in January, so I suppose I have still more than a month to wait for a letter from you. I see your last letter is dated Feb 9th – getting on for two months, & not a word from a soul I know. It's a good job there are plenty of attractions here, or it would be pretty depressing.

I have very little news for you this time. We are still at Wynberg & having a good time. I go into Cape Town several times a week & contrive to enjoy myself exceedingly. The weather remains good, though the winter is rapidly approaching, & by the end of next month it will have broken up completely.

I must send you some views of the place, though I expect you know well enough what Cape Town looks like. Table Mountain is a magnificent pile, but has a wonderful attraction for clouds, which will sometimes cover it all day though the rest of the sky is quite clear. Very often these take the appearance of a table cloth – a white layer covering the flat top & hanging a little way down the sides. The local train & tram services are excellent & the local beauty spots are mostly easy of access. The Cafés, with their balconies & verandahs, are very tempting, though iced drinks have not been reduced to the fine art one would expect in a hot country. Fruit is not extraordinarily plentiful, except grapes, a magnificent bunch of which costs only twopence or threepence.

The general impression now is that we are going back to German East – perhaps fairly soon. I am in no hurry. Out here a private soldier is assumed to be as likely as not a gentleman, & I have become acquainted with one or two very decent people in Cape Town. We hold a corresponding position here to Colonials in England – except that there are fewer of us – the majority of troops being S. African or Australian; & we bear the dignified title of "Imperial Troops". In France I was only British; now I am Imperial, which seems rather grander.

I enclose a snap of myself engaged in the task of potato-peeling which may interest you. Please don't lose it. I am marked with a x as you may have some difficulty in recognising me.

I have a few words to write to Dad so will dry up. Best love to all from

Yours affectionately

Roland

P.S. In case you should not receive my last letter, I will repeat my address – 47655 <u>Pte</u> RDM, No 14 Platoon D Coy 25 R.F. E. African Ex. Fce. C/o G.P.O.

~

[No. 62 – garrison duties at the Castle – a Lance Corporal again – a jaundiced view of South African troops departing for England – a recruiting rally]

Cape Town
13.4.17

Dear Mother,

I'm not sure whether I shall be in time for the mail this week, assuming it to go punctually. We have been rather busy moving & I waited to get a little settled before writing. One Company – ours – has been transferred to the Castle at Cape Town to assist in garrison duties. How long this will last it is of course impossible to say. Up to the present I don't think much of the change. The good point about it is the comfort of the quarters. We are in very comfortable huts, with a mattress & pillow &, in addition to our blankets, two things they <u>call</u> sheets. They seem to be made of some sort of canvas, but with a strong imagination & a little beer before going to bed you can almost fancy you are getting "between the sheets". After the tents, which had several inches of dust on the floor & nothing to prevent it smothering everything you possessed, this is rather luxurious. The bad points are the difficulties of getting out – you could get a pass three days out of four at Wynberg & on the fourth, if you particularly wanted to go out, you went without a pass & nobody seemed to mind, while here, so far as I can see we shall only get out about once a week – the increase in discipline & the strict attention to all the piffling little trifles that constitute three fourths of the evils of army life, & the depression of the locality after the bracing healthiness of the Wynberg hills. The duties are not more arduous if they do not increase them. We provide a guard at the Governor General's residence & a few orderlies &c, which is about all beyond the ordinary fatigues.

I cabled yesterday for £15 & expect a reply in about a fortnight. I don't know if you will know exactly what to do, but it is sufficient to cable that amount through the P.O. to Mountfort, Standard Bank.

To-morrow is the first day of winter & yesterday was 98 ½ ° in the shade. To-day it is much cooler & raining, & the weather has probably broken up for a couple of months. Water is needed very badly. For some time it has been cut off at mid-day.

21/4/17

If I hadn't missed a mail before, I've certainly done it now. I was interrupted to go & guard the "Kenilworth Castle" just in from England. Our duties have been multiplied exceedingly with the result that you never wait for a pass to go out but find a hole in the railings or adopt some similar device, which not only affords you egress whenever you desire, but also gives a "stolen fruit" enjoyment to your evening. However, this doesn't affect me now as I have a permanent pass. The Captn yesterday asked me to take back my stripe & I reluctantly agreed to. So you may once more address me as L/Cpl. They have given me a job in the Company office, but as I have only just taken it on, I can't say yet whether it is any great capture. It gets me out of all other duties, but I never quite fancied clerical work in the Army.

The Castle is about 150-200 years old I believe & is only a barracks. It consists of four walls, with a fortification at each corner, enclosing a couple of courtyards. I don't think there is anything of exceptional interest here.

I don't suppose we shall be here much longer as they have given every man an iron bedstead. If they start to make you really comfortable you can generally take it as a sign you are going to move before long.

I was on guard the other day at the Union Castle quay when a boat was taking S. African troops on board for England. We were on guard all morning, being placed two paces apart across the entrance to the quay to keep back civilians who wanted to see relatives off – rather a rotten job. One lady wept so copiously down my rifle that she made the barrel quite rusty. The train loads of troops bore some amusing chalk signs – as troop trains always do. One was "We are leaving home for King & Country & 3/- a day". The pay question is a sore point out here. The S. Africans think themselves heroic to volunteer at 3/- a day, & the Imperials, with 1/-, tell them what they think about it. Another was covered with various phrases sneering at the "slackers". The writers had been enlisted about a fortnight. Another was "Remember the Lusitania". Someone had been 12 months thinking it over, anyway. When I was on guard while the Kenilworth Castle was in, one of the men on board on picquet[1] on the quay was talking to me during the night. The burden of his conversation was his intense longing for the war to be over so that he could be on his way home again. He said once "You know, it's hard to leave a good home to come out here". Now he had been in the Army exactly eight weeks before leaving England, & was on his way to do garrison duty in India. Yet if I had obeyed my impulse to shove him over the edge of the dock I suppose he would think himself a most injured person.

A big English mail arrived the day before yesterday. Nearly all the original men had half a dozen or more letters, but as yet there is nothing for us.

I'm sorry I've missed the mail. Hope it won't make a very long interval since you last heard.

Very best love to all.

Yours affectionately

Roland

P.S. Yesterday, being St George's Day, they had a wonderful recruiting rally here, advertised for weeks beforehand on every hoarding, cinema screen &c, &c. The proceedings included a great military procession through the town, & every shop, office & business house in the place closed from 10 till 1. The number of recruits the whole turn out brought up was 102.   R

~

---

[1] *piquet*: in this context, a small detachment of troops acting as a guard; English 'picket'. (Also, a wooden or metal stake used to support barbed wire).

[No. 63 – arrival of mail – rumours about future deployment – deteriorating weather – the Kenilworth races – a visit to the theatre]

No 47655 L/Cpl RDM
No 14 Plⁿ D Coy
25th Bⁿ Royal Fus^{rs}
E. African Expdy Force
4th May 1917

Dear Mother,

I have to-day received your first letter dated March 18th. It is just three months since my last letter from you. A big English mail arrived, & we have been devouring Daily Chronicles & London Opinions some six weeks old. You get very little English news in the S. African papers and I learnt for the first time many little things such as the conclusion of the Lloyd George poisoning trial,[1] the absence of newspaper placards &c, &c.

You say in your letter "Dad has told you….." but I have no letter from him. I am sorry to hear he is not very well, & hope by now he is better.

We are still going on in much the same way, & although of course there is no lack of rumour, there is no definite news of what is to happen to us. It seems to be on the cards that we may never see German East; though all the men who have been there pooh-pooh General Smuts' statement that the campaign is nearly over & that no white troops will be required to finish it. So far as the latter is concerned, it is a fact that since Smuts said it large convoys have touched here en route for German East. If we don't go it will be because this Battⁿ is absolutely done up by what it has done there already. A larger party than our draft is being invalided home in a day or two, which leaves the Battⁿ weaker than ever, & nearly all the original men left get periodical doses of fever. Still I shall be very disappointed if there is any truth in the rumour that we shall all be sent back to Europe. Apart from the fact that until the end of the war Africa seems to be a much more desirable spot than Europe, one will look such a fool to have come all this way & not seen anything but Cape Town, even though you may have got to know that rather particularly well.

The weather is getting fairly bad. It is rotten bad luck after having stuck nearly the whole of the English winter to come out here just in time to catch this. We shall be getting up in the dark again soon, & night comes on about 6.30 p.m. already.

A week ago to-day I went to the Kenilworth Races. A good deal of racing goes on about here, & they have rather jolly little meetings. The usual excitement in horse racing is somewhat damped by the fact that all the old hands know to an

---

[1] *Lloyd George poisoning trial*: the widely reported trial in February and March 1917 of the Derbyshire Socialist and anti-war campaigner, Alice Wheeldon, and her alleged associates, for conspiracy to murder Lloyd George whilst he played golf, by shooting him with a poisoned air rifle pellet. Although sentenced to 10 years imprisonment, Wheeldon was released later the same year, following Lloyd George's intervention. (It has now been revealed that the plot was set up by an agent provocateur acting for MI5).

ounce what every horse is worth; with the result that the favourite usually starts with odds on, & pretty often wins.

After the custom of the country, soldiers are free of the course, grand-stand, paddock – in fact everything except the members' enclosure.

Similarly you don't pay to go on the pier or bathe from any of the bathing pavilions.

I saw "Hobson's Choice" at the Opera House the other week – not bad, though a poor Company. They are very badly off for theatres & music halls here – only one of each & both rotten. We are rather unlucky to be at Cape Town; both Johannesburg & Durban (especially the latter) are infinitely pleasanter & more lively.

I duly received your answer to my cable – fifteen days from the date of despatch – not at all bad. What did it cost you? I had deferred rate, 1/3 a word & fifteen bob in all. I hope to goodness they send us up to German East before I want any more, for I am determined not to get any. I came out here to save money, & up to the present without any justification I have spent it with unprecedented lavishness. I've had a good time, but it's lasting too long.

I had my photo taken the other day. I expect it will be a pretty rotten thing, but I'll send you one when I get them.

Was my letter from Sierra Leone much censored? One fellow who described the crush on the boat rather vividly had a reply saying that only half his letter got home, & that very cut about.

I hope I shall get letters from you oftener now. Three months was a dickens of a stretch. What news of Dormor?

Very best love to all,

Yours affectionately

Roland

~

[No. 64 – departure from Cape Town – train journey to Durban – impressions of Durban and its population]

Durban, 17th May 1917

Dear Dad,

Last night I received letters from you & mother dated 1st April. I think there must be one letter from you missing, but the old hands out here reckon that if you receive one third of the letters sent, you are not doing so badly.

We left Cape Town on Saturday morning (12.5.17) by train & arrived here on Tuesday (15.5.17) evening, a very comfortable three days journey. In the S. African trains every compartment is a sleeping compartment for six. On either side the seat makes one bed, the padded back comes up on hinges & makes a second, and an enlarged pack swings down & makes the top one. The journey was naturally very interesting, though we missed one or two parts in the night that I should like to have seen. Bloemfontein I saw in the dim light of dawn, & Bethlehem in dusk of evening, Ladysmith not at all. De Aar, Kroonstat & Pietermaritzburg we reached during the day time & I sent you a p.c. from the second named. The Karroo we ran through mostly in the night, but saw the edge of it next morning. For about a day out from Cape Town the country is the most barren & desolate imaginable – just scrub, covered with small rocks & bare hills, with never a sign of life but a few donkeys & an occasional ostrich. The second day, through the Free State the plains are much more fertile, and on the third, approaching Durban, the vegetation is very rich & the whole district quite beautiful & well cultivated.

Durban is much hotter than Cape Town & the flora is more tropical. The avenue on the sea front is of various sorts of palm trees & tropical plants of many varieties are to be seen in ordinary suburban gardens. The nights are cold (inland as we came through there were severe frosts) but the days are blazing hot & bathing is in full swing. The surf is much finer than on the Peninsula coast, but unfortunately bathing must be restricted to an enclosure on account of sharks.

I shall not see much of Durban as we leave by boat to-morrow for the East. I am sorry as it is in every way a vastly finer place than Cape Town. There are some magnificent hotels & the Municipal buildings are as fine a pile as anything I have seen. There are no cabs but thousands of rickshaws, drawn by Zulus mostly, who get themselves up in a wonderful war paint surmounted by head-dresses of bullock horns & feathers.

I went into the native market yesterday, but should want the pen of a Stevenson to describe what I saw. It is one of the finest native markets going. The coloured population is very large & they have their own police who strut about with knobkerries & look very fierce. I saw one or two strings of beads in the market, but nothing I fancied much. (That remark is for Mother).

Two days is nothing in a place like this. You always feel lost in a new place for the first week. After that you begin to know a few people & start to look around & feel your feet. I was very sorry to leave Cape Town for many things.

We are under canvas at the end of the marine parade. The photos I had done at Cape Town were not ready when we left but I arranged for them to be sent to me by post. They will have to follow me up to German East now, & you won't get one for ages.

I'm keeping pretty fit, but don't like the news from England. Russia has been a damned wash-out from the start. We have rumours of wholesale strikes in England & the prospect is as bad as it can be.

I don't suppose I shall be much too early if I wish Mother many happy returns. Very best love to all.

Your loving son

Roland

P.S. The white population here is nearly all English, unlike Cape Town, where it is Colonial, with a large admixture of Dutch; & the Huts[1] & Recreation Rooms provided for the troops are excellent beyond belief. You can get tea, bread & butter, two eggs, fruit salad & cakes for sixpence. When things get too bad you had better all emigrate.

R.

P.P.S. The total rail journey is about 1258 miles, so you can tell by the time it was pretty slow. They don't go in much for cuttings or embankments but climb up hills & down the other side, winding around often like the horseshoe pass at Llangollen. About 100 miles from Durban you are over 3000 ft above sea level.

R

~

[No. 65]

Durban 19.5.17

Dear Mother,

We sail at 9 a.m. to-morrow Sunday on the "Medic" for German East.

I enclose a photo of myself & another Johnny in a rickshaw. The whole process takes about 2 ½ minutes so it will probably be a sheet of white paper by the time it reaches you. No news since my last. Best love to all.

R.

---

[1] *Huts*: presumably the Young Men's Christian Association (YMCA) huts for recreation and refreshments; often substantial premises which belied the name 'huts'.

Chapter 8

GERMAN EAST AFRICA,
JUNE 1917 – JANUARY 1918
LETTERS 66-77

The 25th (Service) Battalion, Royal Fusiliers (Frontiersmen), returned to active service in May 1917, arriving at the port of Lindi at the beginning of June. Lindi, a settlement of some 4,500 people, 60 miles north of the border with Portuguese East Africa, had been captured from the Germans in September 1916 and had become an increasingly important British base for the campaign against the remaining German forces. Unfortunately, it was situated at the swampy mouth of the Lukuledi River, an area described by one Fusilier as: "undoubtedly the most unhealthy country it was ever our misfortune to enter".[1]

The 25th Royal Fusiliers became part of what was known as the 'Lindi Column', subsequently 'Linforce'. The main focus of their activity was the area to the south of the Rufigi River, inland from Kilwa. By this stage of the war, all the ports in German East Africa had been captured, along with more than a million square miles of German territory, and von Lettow-Vorbeck's forces had been driven into the south-eastern corner of the colony. Although he could count on no more than 9,000 troops, by comparison with more than 50,000 at the disposal of the British, the real strength of the British forces had been greatly reduced by sickness and by the need to protect long lines of communication. In fact, there were only about 13,000 troops available for the advances from Lindi and from the port of Kilwa, some 85 miles to the north. Moreover, the dense bush which covered so much of the colony made the search for the German forces a difficult and dangerous undertaking: "like searching for a needle in a haystack, with a handful of Germans hidden in thousands of square miles of bush" was how one South African soldier described it[2]. Undefeated after three years of fighting, possessed of a better knowledge of the terrain and capable of moving his troops around with greater rapidity than his opponents, von Lettow-Vorbeck remained a formidable foe.

The 25th Royal Fusiliers were soon in action: the Battalion was towed up the River Lukuledi on the night of June 10th for a surprise attack on a German position at Ziwani, eight miles up the estuary of the Lukuledi River. (This is the action described by Roland in Letter 77). In the weeks that followed, the climate and conditions proved as much of an adversary as the Germans and, by August, Roland was recovering in Dar-es-Salaam from dysentery. He therefore missed the start of the main campaign in July, when three columns from Kilwa, under General Beves, began to push the German forces south, whilst another three

---

[1] Captain Angus Buchanan, M.C., "Three Years of War in East Africa" ; John Murray, 1919.
[2] Deneys Reitz in "Trekking On", Faber & Faber, 1933 – quoted in "Tip and Run" by Edward Paice, Weidenfeld & Nicolson, 2007.

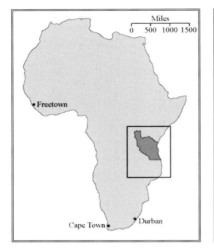

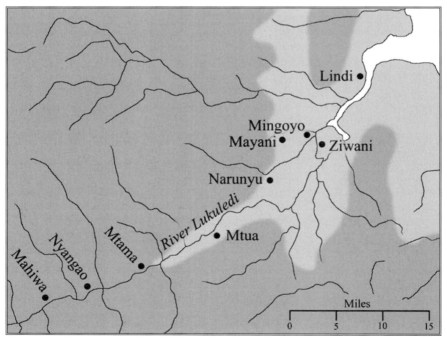

The Lukuledi River, June 1917 – January 1918

Letters 66-77

columns, under General O'Grady, were ordered to force their way inland from Lindi and cut off the German retreat from the Kilwa front. It was the start of almost five months of continual fighting.

By the end of August, Roland had returned to Lindi and was waiting to go up the line and, in October, he was once more out in the bush. A major action with the Germans, on October 17th and 18th, and the ravages of the climate made serious inroads into the 25th Battalion's strength and, by the end of 1917, it was finished as a fighting force. Roland, like many of the survivors, was mentally and physically exhausted. In December, he was in hospital in Durban, convalescing after an attack of fever, and it was from hospital that the last of his surviving letters was written on January 6th, 1918.

∼

Letters 66 – 70 were written from the Battalion camp at Lindi on the estuary of the Lukuledi River. Illness soon took a heavy toll of the Battalion: on June 26th there were only 155 men on parade – the rest were sick or in hospital – and the Senior Medical Officer believed that only 36 of the 155 were actually fit enough to go on column.

∼

[No. 66 – arrival of 'gigantic mail' – Dormor – malaria – bandas]

P.S. Have you any word of Spencer?[1] East Africa, 4th July 1917
I suppose as he was a friend of mine he
hasn't got much chance of coming through.

Dear Mother,

A gigantic mail arrived yesterday and by it I received the following: a letter from Dad dated 14th March, in answer to my first despatched at Sierra Leone; a letter from Dad dated 17th April, telling me of the receipt of my cable & of Dormor's & Geoff's arrival; a letter from you dated 24th April giving me the same news in greater detail, & enclosing a note re money from Dad; and lastly a long letter from Gwyneth dated 25th April telling me of her visit to Wellington. I should imagine that these together with the ones I have already acknowledged – two in S. Africa & Dad's of 29th April (curiously enough) by the mail before this – make up about all you have written up to the end of April, so I am not doing so badly. I trust my letters home are being equally fortunate.

I was amazed to hear of Dormor's visit home; I had no idea that leave was granted from Salonica, though by jove it was about time he had a holiday. It was something of a surprise too, to learn he had malaria, for I did not imagine it was at all prevalent in that theatre of war. As you may imagine, I know about all there is to know about it now – with the exception of what it feels like to have it; & I have little doubt my ignorance in that one respect will soon be remedied. Why I have escaped so far I haven't the faintest idea. This coast is a fever stricken hole & June & July are supposed to be about the two worst months. However, I pump quinine[2] into myself & keep smiling.

Except to shift camp from one side of the village to the other we have done nothing exciting since I last wrote, & I have no news at all. I hang out in a banda now. That same is a hut constructed of grass woven into a framework of boughs. It's comfortable enough, but the mosquitoes are rather partial to it & it is unadvisable to sleep without a net.

By this same mail I received a letter from Aunt Lyd dated March 12th & sent on from Dover, & one from Auntie Annie dated 27th April. I am very pleased indeed that both Aunt Lyd & Marie are now better, the former being with Maud at Louth & the latter at Oxford.

I have seen a newspaper dated as late as May 1st but don't gather that there is any likelihood of any immediate conclusion of the war.

Very best love to all,

Yours affectionately

Roland

---

[1] *Spencer*: presumably, Frank Spencer, a close friend of the family. See photograph on Page 82.
[2] *quinine*: the bitter tasting anti-malaria drug extracted from the bark of the cinchon tree.

[No. 67 – character of a 'personal slave' – insect life – increasing grasp of Swahili]

4th July
1917

My dear Gwyneth,

I was delighted to receive your long letter narrating your adventures in Shropshire. I don't think I have heard from anyone in that locality for over two years. I am rather looking forward to my first visit there après la guerre.

I wish you were here to see something of the weird & wonderful sights that interest one so much at first, but very speedily lose their strangeness. The barbarian on his native hearth is distinctly more picturesque than his collared & coated brother in Durban or Cape Town. My own personal slave is a rum blighter. I believe he must be something of a knut[1] in his own family circle; he is always after old bits of cloth for his personal adornment, which he thinks of miles before his physical comfort; & he struts to & fro from the village with an elaborate knobkerry. His great disadvantage is that he has been recently married, & pesters unceasingly for errands to the village which will give him an opportunity of calling upon his better half. If he is to be believed (which I am afraid he is not always) she is a very fastidious young lady, for on more than one occasion when we have given him his grub he has complained that his wife, if you please, doesn't like rice; can't he have mealie meal?

The insect life reminds me of that rather piffling book of Wells' "The Food of the Gods"; everything seems to have swelled to about fifty times its ordinary size. Butterflies are bigger than the palm of your hand, grasshoppers are as fat as your middle finger, and there is a delightful little creature exactly resembling in features an English wire worm, but as long and thick as an ordinary black ruler.

My fluency in the aristocratic Swahili language increases daily. When you have mastered "Lapana mzuri" the equivalent of the Anglo-French "no bon" it is half the battle.

I was very sorry, when I heard of the grand rendezvous that took place on the Tuesday of Dormor's arrival, that I should have been so far away. We must have a still grander one some day.

Very best love from

Your affec[te] brother

Roland

---

[1] *knut*: someone taking exaggerated care over his appearance; from a very popular 1914 song "Gilbert the Filbert", sung by a West End Actor, Basil Hallam Radford, known to theatre-goers as Basil Hallam: I am Gilbert, the Filbert
　　　　The knut with a k,
　　　　The pride of Piccadilly
　　　　And blasé roue!
Radford subsequently joined up and served as a kite-balloon observer but was killed in 1916 when his balloon cable snapped and his parachute failed to open when he jumped.

[No. 68]

East Africa,
12th July 1917

Dear Dad,

I received a short letter from you yesterday dated 6th May. Very glad to hear you are all keeping well, & hope you are not yet quite starved. There is sort of impression here, I don't know why, that prices in England are having a slight tendency to go down. I hope this is so.

I have no news to add to my letters of a few days ago to Mother & Gwyneth. We are perpetually expecting to start on trek & not starting, though I don't think we can delay much longer. We hear, in the scrappy, unsatisfactory way of wireless news, of a rotten air-raid on London. Hope Vin & Annie didn't get too much of it.

I still in some mysterious way escape fever. Hope you are getting my letters pretty regularly. Two months each way seems to be about the minimum now. Trust Dormor is "safe back in the trenches". What news of Geoff? Best love to all.

R.

~

[No. 69 – an anniversary – precautions against malaria – a new servant]

East Africa. 19th July 1917

Dear Mother,

Just a line to catch the next mail. There is no news, & I have received no further mail from you. To-day is the anniversary of my landing in England after my wound, & of my motor ride through the city in all the glory of my five days beard & dirt. Nothing more has happened to us yet. The sun begins to get very powerful at mid-day, being on its southward journey. I am still keeping fit – no fever or anything yet. I really can't understand it. For the last week they have had us on a daily dose of 20 grains of quinine, an enormous quantity for men temporarily clear of fever. I find eight grains about my mark. I have sacked the boy I last told you of & now possess a specimen answering to the name of – as far as I can make it out – "Mahmud", though he hasn't yet produced an enchanted sword to scatter & slay the misbelieving & black horde of cares & sorrows that infest the soul[1], but contents himself with cadging cigarettes. Hope you are all well, & that I shall hear from you again soon. Very best love to all.

R.

P.S. If my other letters should have miscarried, my last from you is May 6th – a short note from Dad.　　　　R.

---

[1] *"Mahmud"…an enchanted sword etc*: from the 'Rubaiyat of Omar Khayyam'.

The "small move" mentioned in Letter 70 was to Mayani and was made by 20 officers and over 300 men on July 26th.

~

[No. 70 – a move up-country – health]

East Africa
25th July 1917

Dear Mother,

Just a line to wish you many happy returns of the day. You understand of course that you are to receive your present from Dad.

I have no news yet to add to my last few notes. To-morrow we are making a small move, I believe, a little way inland. The Germans up country have had a nasty bump or two recently[1], & those here can't be feeling too comfortable. With a bit of luck they should all be cornered reasonably soon, but they are as slippery as eels – as elusive as shrimps in a sea-pool.

There is no more mail from you. The last is a short note from Dad dated May 6th, rather a long time ago & I hope you have all been going strong since then. I am still keeping fit – have got so thin that the roaring lion, malaria, mistakes me for a cocoa-nut palm – but don't mind how soon we get back to a civilised climate.

Very best love to all

R.

~

Roland did not last long on trek; he fell ill with dysentery and was evacuated to Dar-es-Salaam. One factor mentioned in the Battalion war diary that appears to have contributed to the incidence of dysentery was the inability to boil water – presumably for fear of disclosing positions to the enemy. As a result of his illness, Roland missed two engagements. The first was on August 3rd, near Mingoyo, where the Battalion suffered 26 casualties, approximately 10% of the force involved. The second engagement was fought at Narunyu; this started on August 18th, lasted for five days and resulted in a further five casualties. The purpose of these operations was to help prepare the way for a general advance in September. However, they met with more vigorous opposition than had been anticipated.

---

[1] *The Germans up country have had a nasty bump or two recently*: presumably a reference to the initial success enjoyed by the British columns advancing from Kilwa, which had forced the Germans to retreat southwards.

[No. 71 – hospital again – the march up-country – onset of sickness – stretchered out – boat journey – medical treatment – hospital ship to Dar-es-Salaam – mail – reading]

East Africa,
12th August 1917

Dear Mother,

Once more I am appearing in all the bravery of a hospital blue suit; though not, alas! in the dear old Mile End Road, nor boasting of any honourable scar. Something more than a fortnight ago I was unfortunate enough to succumb to an attack of dysentery, from which however, I am happily practically recovered. The incident has brought me one or two new experiences.

As I foretold in my last letter we got on track the next day *[July 26th]*, & moved some dozen miles inland to a position in a rubber plantation *[at Myani]* where we built ourselves bandas, & settled down generally to be as comfortable as might be. The march was pleasant enough, as we started very early, & broke the back of it before the extreme heat of the day. One halt was in a grove of coconut palms, & every nigger in the column was employed in shying nuts down; they were just ripe & the milk is gorgeous.

I had not been up to the mark for some days, but thought that the trek would do me good; it had the opposite effect though, & the next day I was compelled to go sick. Two days later I was worse, & then they detained me in the Aid Post. The next morning *[July 30th]* early a batch of eight of us were despatched under escort to the nearest advanced hospital. Five miles of bush track on a stretcher is not one of the most delightful journeys imaginable, even in health. The bearers are four niggers, who each take a handle, sometimes on their shoulder, sometimes on their head (the nigger's pet way of porterage; I don't believe there's any limit to what he can carry, once you can cajole or coerce him to get it on his head); & away they go merrily, without any regard whatever to their respective altitudes or the nature of the ground, so that one moment you clutch dizzily whatever is handiest to prevent you slipping off on to your head, while the next one all but encompasses your destruction in a violent roll to starboard. My boys seemed fired with an earnest though misplaced zeal to head the procession; we started last but one but finished up second. It is so rare for boys to get a move on of their own accord except when a rifle is fired within five miles of them that I hadn't the heart to check them; but the jolting was awful. We arrived at the hospital in due course, & I got very comfortably to bed. I was marked for transfer however, & two hours later started off again – by stretcher to the river, & thence by lighter down to the coast to the hospital at the place we started on track from *[Lindi]*. Here I remained some five days, until a week ago to-day, & here, though very weak, I began to mend. There is some stuff called emetine[1] they inject for this complaint, & this I had for four days. My diet was three cups of milk a day for about ten days. So, like Cassius, I wore a lean and hungry look, & my wrist watch, strapped

---

[1] *emetine*: a drug extracted from the root of the ipecac plant and used in the treatment of amoebic dysentery; administering it hypodermically, rather than orally, reduced the likelihood of nausea.

in its accustomed hole, slipped up and down my arm. One night I had an injection of morphia – the first time I have ever had anything of that kind. I shall never be able to think badly of morphia maniacs in future. Almost immediately came a delightful unearthly feeling of peace stealing gently through every vein, & all the fatigue & the pain & the tiredness-of-life just faded away like breath from a mirror.

Here I was marked for evacuation to the base Hospital at Dar-es-Salaam[1]. I went on board the Hospital Ship last Sunday, a week ago to-day, & was on board four days, though the actual time of travel is little more than 24 hours. We waited some time before sailing, payed a long call at a port en route, & again waited to disembark. I arrived at the hospital from which I am now writing about midday Friday, Aug 10th. It is a very large building, very roomy & cool. I am convalescent now & shall be pretty comfortable here, I dare say.

I had one bit of bad luck on the boat – I was put on chicken diet & got well too quickly. This was unfortunate, as otherwise I should probably not have come ashore here at all, but gone straight on board a hospital boat for S. Africa. I am on a mince diet here, & have an appetite like a horse, I am ceasing to look so infernally goggle-eyed, but am still inclined towards the cadaverous. I feel very well, however. One other experience before we leave the subject. At the other hospital, for the first time in some 20 years I had my face and hands washed for me. I don't know why children object to it so – I thought it rather pleasant.

Just before leaving Lindi Hospital I was fortunate enough to receive a large mail. By it I had two letters from you dated 23rd May & 3rd June, one from Dad dated 14th June & one from Gwyneth from Bournemouth dated 23rd May. You tell me of Geoff's adventures in the trenches, Hilda & Norah's confirmation & Pepys Diary. Dad & Gwyneth I am writing to separately. Now that I am away from the Battalion I expect I won't get my letters, or only after much delay. I suppose my letters are taking 2 months to reach you? From here they may take a little less.

There was a library of sorts on the boat. I read "A Study in Shadows" by W. J. Locke, "A Knight on Wheels" by Ian Hay, & Borrows "Gypsies of Spain". The first was wanting in cleverness I thought, except for the title; which is excellent. It is just the impression that the book leaves with you, of looking back down a vista of various shades of gloom, but with no relief of light at all. The second is very readable but <u>so</u> like the rest. All Ian Hay's heroes are like peas in a pod. The Gypsies of Spain is too much of a treatise & too little of a narrative to afford many glimpses of Borrow's real inimitable self.

Well, I must write notes to Dad & Gwyneth. I hope you are well & not feeling too much the pinch of war. I haven't seen a later English paper than June 1st, but I suppose there's a war still. Very best love to all from

Yours affectionately

Roland.

---

[1] *Dar-es-Salaam*: the former capital of German East Africa, which had been captured by British forces in September 1916.

By late August Roland had been discharged from hospital and had returned to Lindi.

~

[No. 72 – discharge from hospital – detail camp – return to Lindi]

East Africa,
Aug 26th 1917 (Sunday)

Dear Mother,

A very brief & hurried note. I was discharged from hospital at Dar es Salam six days ago. I spent three days in a detail camp[1] there & was rather sorry it was no longer for the place still retains symptoms of civilisation. You could get a supper in the evening for a rupee & a half & several cafes sold cakes such as you in England are beginning almost to lose recollection of. One evening I went to a cinema show at the YMCA & saw "Charlie's Night Out". I then embarked on a little Japanese boat called the "Chow Tai" & in 48 hours was back here – the same old spot. The sea was very choppy, but I think I am beginning to become something of a sailor. Arrived here yesterday & am going forward up the line to-day. Feeling very well. Weather getting hotter than ever, sun at midday exceedingly powerful. No more letters from you. I think some have gone to Daressalam since I left. Hope you are all well. Very best love to all.

R.

~

On September 23rd, the 25th Royal Fusiliers moved out of camp and became part of a large-scale operation against German positions based on Narunyu and Mtua. A force from Lindi, now under the command of General Beves, and which included the Royal Fusiliers, advanced south-west. Simultaneously, a British force from Kilwa pushed south and, on September 27th, compelled the Germans to abandon their camp at Nahungu and retreat towards the Lukuledi River. As operations continued, it seemed as though the superior manpower and supplies of the British would drive the Germans from the area. However, there was to be a major setback in mid-October.

~

---

[1] *a detail camp*: a base camp.

[No. 73 – missing letters – life on trek]

East Africa,
5th Oct. 1917

Dear Dad,

I have just received your letter of 1st August, written apparently at a moment when the oppression of the war was bearing rather heavily upon you. I hope things are actually a little brighter than you depict. We are rather given to understand from such scant news as reaches us here that conditions at home are rapidly improving in every way. I hope it is so.

This letter (1st Aug.) is the first I have received from any of you since those dated about 15th June, when I heard from Gwyneth about her trip to Bournemouth &c, so how you fared or what happened in that interval I can only conjecture. I understand it has been officially announced that mails for Mesopotamia & G.E.A. dated June & July have been lost at sea, which would account for some of your missing letters. I cannot but think, nevertheless, that there are still some in this country which I have not yet received. I know at any rate that my former O.C. Coy, Capt Page, wrote me a letter from S. Africa, to which he was invalided on being wounded, which should have arrived two mails ago, but of which I have up to the present seen nothing.

We are still well out in the bush, & life is not exactly a continuous whirl of pleasure. We trek around, sometimes stopping in one place a few days, sometimes for one night only, but always well on the heels of the Hun, who still has plenty of kick left in him. A change of clothing caught us up the other day for which I was very thankful, having begun to renew my acquaintance with some close personal friends whose companionship I first enjoyed in France & whose presence when I came home on leave caused you so much alarm. Haven't read anything for 50 years. There are no lights allowed on this stunt, & at sunset, if you are not on outpost, there is no alternative but to go to bed, where, when fatigue obliterates the noise of the five hundred billion different varieties of insect, & the croaking of the bull frogs, & the somnolent snorts & groans of the niggers, you may go to sleep. Out here, thank goodness, they rarely fight at night.

Many happy returns to Gwyneth on her birthday. I hope she gets my present safely. To-morrow, Dormor is 30! Mon Dieu, but time flies.

I am still keeping fit, & have not yet had fever. Mirabile dictu. I wonder why.

Very best love to all from

Your affectionate son,

Roland

~

On October 17th and 18th, 1917, the 25th Royal Fusiliers were involved in the bloodiest battle of the campaign, fought around Mahiwa and Nyangao, some 45 miles up the Lukuledi River. The action had begun on October 15th, when Nigerian troops, who were part of the advance from Kilwa, found themselves cut off by German troops in the vicinity of Mahiwa. Over the next few days, British forces made repeated attempts to break through to the beleaguered Nigerians. On October 17th, two British columns from Lindi began to dislodge the German askari from their entrenchments on a ridge south-west of Nyangao. Despite a German counter-attack, contact was finally made with the surviving Nigerians on October 18th. However, another ferocious counter-attack was launched by the Germans and the 25th Royal Fusiliers, who were trying to fill the gaps that had emerged between the two British columns, felt its full weight and suffered badly. In the words of the regimental history: "the Fusiliers were cut to pieces", their strength reduced from 120 men to fewer than 50. It was the Battalion's last battle of the war.

If Roland was involved in this action, as appears likely, then he did well to survive it. However, he makes no direct reference to the battle in Letter 74, which appears to have been written from camp, presumably at Lindi. (The Battalion war diary for this period has not survived). He makes a brief reference to "our big scrap" in Letter 76 but, unfortunately, he does not provide any detail.

Both sides lost heavily in the fighting around Mahiwa and Nyangao. The Germans had to abandon their positions north of the Lukuledi River but the British troops now needed rest and recuperation, their offensive potential blunted for the time being.

~

[No. 74 – an unending war – Christmas wishes]

East Africa
25th Oct.

Dear Mother,

I have just written to Dad, but as this is my Xmas letter I thought I would put a note in for you. It is, of course, certain now that there is no possibility of being at home. What a tiny while ago it seems since I was writing to say I wouldn't be home for last Xmas, but hoped to be for this. Now we have to begin hoping for 1918. This is all very well; but the years are mounting up, & I am beginning to wonder rather anxiously when the end is going to be. Here are all the best years of my life being spent in unfitting myself for my job. And still there is no sign of an end. The news from France seems to be good, but how much nearer a conclusion does it bring us? Out here it's much the same. The Germans are certainly more or less cornered, but fight like rats in a trap, & have to be driven back every inch of the way. There never was such fighting in the country as there has been for the last three months; in spite of Smuts' beautiful declaration[1] about half a year or more ago. His remarks upon the use of white troops carried about an equal amount of truth.

However, this has nothing to do with Xmas. I hope you will have as good a time as possible. I have asked Dad to see about some presents, though, I fear, rather late in the day.

I am well, but am afraid I am beginning to get this cursed climate into my bones. The heat gets burdensome out in this confounded bush, & civilisation seems too far away ever to get back to.

I hope Dad is better now, & the children have contracted no further complaints. With best love & all good wishes for Xmas from

Yours affectionately,

Roland

P.S. Many thanks for the photo. It is, of course, excruciatingly bad.

~

The absence of the relevant Battalion war diary prevents the precise identification of the location at which Letter 75 was written.

~

[No. 75 – a 'swagger banda' and the Sergeants' Mess – Acting Company Quartermaster Sergeant – hotter weather – an elusive rainy season]

East Africa.
15th Nov.

Dear Mother,

I really am not sure at the moment whether I answered the letters I received by the last mail or not. I see I have one from Norah dated 26th August, one from Dad dated 23rd August, & one from an old trench pal re-addressed by you on Aug 24th. These are the latest mails I have, & as it is nearly a fortnight since I received them I cannot say positively whether I replied or not.

There is, I am afraid, no further excuse for my not having written for some little time than the procrastinating frame of mind induced by the climate, for we are not now in the active part of the fighting, & the days of persistent tracking are

---

[1] *Smuts' beautiful declaration*: presumably the claim made by General Smuts in January 1917 that the back of German resistance in East Africa had been broken and that the campaign would be brought to an end within a few months. Smuts also stated his intention to replace white troops with black. See also Letter 63.

past – at least we thought they had until the day before yesterday, when, having spent many days in building substantial bandas with grass beds & biscuit-box tables, we received an order at 7 p.m. to be packed up & move on at 4 a.m. the next morning. We had formed a Sergeants Mess & built a swagger banda with tables for four & all the latest conveniences. For the opening night we invited all the officers to dinner & the menu would have surprised you. The officers duly arrived to dinner bringing with them the information that in about 9 hours time we should have to get up in the dark, leave our delightful banda & Mess & lump all our stuff away into the bush again. I forgot to explain – lest the "we" should puzzle you, that I am at the moment an Acting Company Quartermaster Sergeant, which is, I think you will agree, one of the longest & most imposing titles in the Army, & which is used to represent a lance corporal disguised with three stripes & a crown, employed to reduce the books & rations of the Company to the greatest possible state of confusion in the period of time allowed him before they find the right man for the job. Of course, sometimes the real C.Q.M.S. comes back before things are in a genuine muddle (though it doesn't take long) but I don't think that's fair, really. So you will please continue to address me as usual.

At the last camp a lion used to come & serenade us at night. Numerous donkeys also used to uplift their voice in song. Here, except for the usual grasshopper chorus, which you can never get clear of, but which is seldom louder than a locomotive blowing off steam at ten paces, the nights are fairly quiet.

The days are getting warmish now. At midday the sun is exactly overhead & its penetrative power is surprising. You need about a foot of grass on the roof of a banda before you dare take your helmet off. The climate is mysterious. A rainy season was supposed to be going to start early in September. At the beginning of September however it was decided that the rains did not commence until the end of the month. About half way through the month, the rainy season was spoken of as due at the end of October. Then everyone forgot all about it, until one day they discovered it was already November & the rains had not made their appearance. So the latest information is that the rains start (a) at the beginning of January (b) at the end of March (c) do not start at all.

In my last letter, which was supposed to be my Xmas letter & will probably reach you about the middle of January I asked Dad to cash my second cheque *[illegible]* for Xmas presents & general festivities. Possibly I may be in a position to cable before Xmas, & if so I will do so.

Please thank Norah for her long letter. I will try & answer it one of these days. Hope you are all well & not too much oppressed by the war. I keep pretty fit, in some remarkable manner which I don't profess to understand. Very best love to all,

Roland

~

[No. 76 – the 'big scrap' – further attack of fever – return to Dar-es-Salaam via Lindi – a 'rotten' five days as Company QMS – recovery at Durban – depletion of Company strength during campaign – a dull Christmas – hospital fire – speculation about Battalion's future – views on black and Indian troops – the original 25th Battalion]

No. 3 General Hospital,
Durban.
1. 1. 18.

Dear Dad,

I am starting the New Year well by writing to you for the first time for ages. It hasn't been altogether my fault, but I will try & make amends now by telling you everything I can think of, regardless of time & note-paper.

First, I may say I have received all your letters up to No. 10, which is an Xmas greeting from you all, for which I thank you very much. It is post-marked 17th Oct, & is as late a communication as I have received from any one. Being where I am I don't expect to get any more for ages.

Now for the narrative. You heard of me last in the standing camp in which we spent somewhere about a month after our big scrap[1] on Oct 18th, when over 60% of the Battalion were casualties. It was here I began to get small attacks of fever which worried me very little as I threw them off with the utmost ease. Anon came the glad news that the war was practically over, & about the beginning of December we began to track back to the coast. My recollections of that track are not pleasant. Every day, as soon as we got into camp I went down with fever & every night I pulled round sufficiently to start again the next morning. At length we reached Myngoyo from whence we proceeded by lighter down the Lukuledi to Lindi. Of my Company, which, with the reinforcements that reached us in Sept^r & Octr had reached a total strength of over 200 in E. Africa, seventeen marched into the Detail Camp at Lindi on the night of Dec 3rd. We stayed a few days in Lindi & I had fever most of the time. Then we embarked on the Chow Tai – the same little Chink boat that carried me back to Lindi after dysentery – for Dar-es-Salam. Here we were joined up by numbers of men raked out from hospital at Dar-es-Salam, Morogoro, Nairobi, & other cushy places & began to look something like a Battⁿ again. Here, too, I had the rottenest five days I have had in the country. I was still acting as the Quartermaster Sergeant of the Coy, & the amount of work was appalling. Every man had to be completely refitted with everything of which he had become deficient during the campaign; the Company was paid out; they raked up an old canteen rebate question from Cape Town days; & as we expected to sail any minute everything had to be done in such a frantic hurry as to preclude any possibility of doing it properly or systematically. The Regimental Stores added to the confusion by getting in supplies bit by bit instead of all together; & the confusion was worse confounded by batches of men arriving from hospital every morning & evening; of course deficient of everything. Thus, when you had the Whole Company completely equipped except with entrenching-tool-handle-

---

[1] *our big scrap*: the battle fought on October 17th-18th at Mahiwa and Nyangao (see background notes on pages 133-135 and 144).

carriers, puttees, hair-brushes & jack-knives, a batch would arrive from Morogoro sans everything. You would put in an indent to Regimental Stores for all their requirements & when you went to draw the articles, you would find included with them entrenching-tool-handle-carriers, puttees, hair-brushes & jack-knives, but only for the rest of the Company & not for the new arrivals being supplied on a previous Indent, while in addition there would now be a deficiency of Field Service Caps, braces, & bayonet frogs. You can imagine – or rather I don't think you can – the state of affairs by about the third day. There were scores of minor annoyances, too, such as men going back into hospital & returning you all their equipment a couple of hours after you had issued it to them; the boots & caps being all the wrong sizes; & half the damned fools who came out in October not knowing what they wanted until, after you had given them all they asked for, they found they hadn't got it.

So I was worried nearly off my head – principally I think because I was really getting in rather a low way. I had stuck the country better than any other man in the Company except one; but now I was physically & mentally – especially the latter – completely worn out. The horrible, infernal climate had got me right down & was just going to jump on me when we sailed South on the "Ingoma" on Dec[r] 13th. Even here there was no rest, for they started to issue Serge clothing, underpants, cardigan jackets & other preparations for England. I was thankful, whole-heartedly thankful, when, on arriving at Durban on Dec[r] 19th, I was in the middle of a bad attack of fever & was taken straight to hospital. It meant, what I wanted worse than I ever have before, a complete rest; & it further meant ceasing to be a Q.M.S. which is a thing accursed; & becoming once more a light-hearted, careless Corporal – did you know I had another stripe?

It took three days to get my temperature to remain permanently somewhere in the position of normal, & since then it has not shown the least tendency to stray. I don't think I shall hear much more of fever; it doesn't seem natural to my constitution; although the first blood test I have had taken revealed every kind of malaria germ nearly that ever was heard of – but the blood was taken when my temperature was in the neighbourhood of a hundred & – something fearful, I forget what. That it is not natural to my constitution the fact that I had absolutely none until November, combined with a few statistics which can hardly be censorable now the war is over, will show, I think. We landed at Lindi on May 29th; my Company was 118 strong. A fortnight later we went on our expedition up the Lukuledi, briefly reported in the Mirror of June 25th (about) as "Surprise Landing in E. Africa". A week after our return 70 of the 118 were in hospital with fever. After their first attack a few stuck out pretty well & when on July 25th we started on our track inland, we were fairly strong again. At the beginning of Sept[r] we were less than 30. In the middle of Sept[r] were only 20, & confidently expected to be recalled South. On 18th Sept we received a draft of 50 men & the news that 50 more were on their way up. They were mostly conscripts, & a measly lot at that. A month later we went into action about 25 strong! The second batch of 50 arrived in the middle of the action but did not go into it. So once more we had a handful of men to play with. When we had been in the standing camp a month we were down to 20 again. As I said before, we finished up in Lindi seventeen strong, out of a total of over 200, one hundred of whom had been less than 3 months in the country. So you may judge for yourself what a pestilential, fever-stricken God-forsaken hole it was our luck to strike, & how heartily thankful I ought to be for such a light escape.

I don't suppose you have a large scale map of GEA, it certainly isn't worth while getting one, but should you ever come across anything of the kind, the line of advance of our (Lindi) column was Mingoyo, Mtua, Mtama, & Nyangao. Here the big scrap took place, &, Massassi & Mahenge both having fallen, the Germans bunked off into Portuguese East[1] – at least such as did not surrender. We hardly struck any of these places however, except coming back, for it was always our luck to be doing flanking movements through virgin bush & other pretty little stunts of that sort. We were driving the Germans before us all the time. They even held Mingoyo when we landed at Lindi, until our expedition up the river drove them out.

Well, we will leave E. Africa temporarily & come to Durban. As I said, I was pretty rotten for three days, & since then have been mending rapidly. While I was bad my head was in a very peculiar state. I couldn't sleep because I had only to close my eyes to behold a wonderful cinematograph show; the weirdest scenes imaginable quite beyond description presented themselves to me unceasingly until I was glad to open my eyes again to see a few normal things. Huge armies marching over vast plains, gigantic naval battles, colossal buildings in great cities, & then little hovels, weird dells & rural nooks, by-ways & corners – an eternal panorama that made you feel quite giddy. I had a dose of chloral[2] one night & all that happened was some horrible nightmare for about two hours, & then wakefulness & the same old bioscope show. So I tried what I should have done if I had been treating myself – about a quart of water to allay my thirst; resulting in a healthy sleep for an hour, a good perspiration, & a low temperature for the first time in 18 hours.

However, as I say, fever is a thing of the past. Christmas day was rather dull – just an extra good dinner & nothing more – except for a few evergreens & flags scattered about the ward. I always thought Xmas in hospital was one long orgie of merriment & was rather disappointed. We had a few small gifts from the Durbanites, of which the most useful was 10/- each from the Turf Club. There was considerably more excitement on the 27th when the tent I was in, consisting of three marquees joined together, & containing about 30 patients, caught fire about one o'clock in the morning & in about ten minutes was burnt to the ground. Nobody was hurt, but the difficulty was to find accommodation for us, the hospital being very full; & we sat around in a lettuce patch in pyjamas & slippers while they discussed the situation. For me they found a very comfortable bed in the Sgt Major's tent; but most of them had to share the few mattresses that were rescued from the fire on the floor of the mess tent; a hard bed, but perhaps a shade better than a bed of lettuces. The next day they scattered us among various wards.

---

[1] *the Germans bunked off into Portuguese East*: on November 25th, 1917, von Lettow-Vorbeck's remaining forces crossed the Rovuma River and entered Portuguese East Africa. Here they were able to continue their resistance; they finally surrendered on November 25th, 1918, a year to the day after crossing the Rovuma, and two weeks after the signing of the Armistice in Europe.

[2] *chloral*: a colourless, oily liquid used as a sedative; made from chlorine and acetaldehyde.

I am now in what was a drill hall. It contains xteen rows of beds with y^2 $^b/_a$ beds[1] in each row. It is like being in a room where two mirrors face each other – you see beds & beds stretching away into the dim distance until the rows all meet at infinity.

The people I met at Durban last time have been to see me; & I have not wanted for cigarettes, fruit & literature. Since I have begun to get about a bit I have been to see them, & had some whisky & soda, & been a very decent motor ride.

The Battalion sailed from here on the 27th & where they have gone to I have not yet heard. They have either gone straight to England or they are staying at Wynberg. If the former you can expect to see me before the year is much older; if the latter it is of course possible that some or all of us may be sent straight to Egypt or Mesopotamia or somewhere; but the general belief is that they are bound for Blighty. I must say that except to see you all I have no desire to come to England at present. The newspapers don't make it sound a bit inviting; after getting into Frontiersman habits I don't fancy the barrack-square; & I doubt if my constitution is sufficiently undermined to save me from France. However, it's all on the knees of the Gods.

Well I think I must chuck this for to-night. I shall post it to-morrow afternoon, but if I have time during the morning I will add a few more items of interest. In case I don't, I wish to repeat that I am perfectly well & strong again now – absolutely as fit as ever. It was only when I was quite tired out that the fever could get hold of me at all. By Jove, I <u>was</u> tired. I was getting nervous for my disposition too. It's a fairly happy one, really, but towards the end I was so irritable I couldn't speak civilly to my own pals & I don't think I <u>laughed</u> from the end of November until my fourth day in hospital. But I've been making up for it since.

2. 1. 18.

Just a few more lines.

The varieties of troops with whom we came in (sometimes too close) contact during the campaign were almost endless. There were numerous Batt[ns] of King's African Rifles – black troops from British East & various parts of Africa. They wore khaki drill tunics & shorts with a small drill cloth cap, & drilled very smartly & fought well. Some of them were quite old soldiers with several ribbons & long service stripes; but there were one or two Batt[ns] wholly of recruits. The remaining black troops were principally Nigerians. They wore a similar uniform with a big straw hat or else a little woollen cap. They fought like tigers & were popularly supposed to eat their victims if they got half a chance. Indians were there of all shades & degrees of intelligence, Cawnpores, Kashmirs, Punjabis, Baluchis, Barakpores – there was no end to them. They mostly didn't distinguish themselves as infantry but their mountain batteries were about the smartest turn-outs I've ever struck. They also shone conspicuously at all sorts of pioneer & engineering work. Then there were some West Indians who wore sun-helmets &

---

[1] *Xteen rows…*: in other words, a very large number of beds.

thought no small beer of themselves, always speaking English if there was a white man anywhere around. We were the only Imperial Infantry Batt[n]. The S. African Infantry had a few men up there, & the remaining whites were principally artillery – we had a few howitzers & a big naval gun – & motor transport. The porters were collected from all over the place, the Germans having collared all the local savages; & were often an unholy nuisance, men of one tribe refusing to eat with men of another, or even use the same cooking pots. I had some little experience of them while I was Q.M.S. You may be awfully keen on the "man & a brother" theory in peace time, but on active service you are bound to come to the conclusion that the only argument which really appeals to a raw African savage is a thick stick carefully & firmly applied. I don't suppose you can quite picture me nigger driving, can you?

At first every nigger looks like the next one. But it is remarkable how quickly, when living amongst them, you learn to discern their individuality. Before long you can discriminate between them as easily as among white men; can recognise after an interval a boy you may have seen only once before; & even criticise their appearance, recognising one as a handsome nigger & another as an ugly one where at first the whole crowd looked as ugly as sin.

The original 25th were a tough lot, but there are not many left now. They came from everywhere under the sun; & the conversation of a group of them dealt not only with the pubs in Walworth High Street – as most military conversations do; or something similar – but with the four corners of the world. Of the few friends I made this is a sample – one, after the Boer War, managed hotels in Bloemfontein & Buluwayo, & then went to the Argentine as a commercial traveller for Johnny Walker; one, also after the Boer War, went into the glass trade in Paris; & fought during the first six months of the war with the French Foreign Legion; one came over from the farthest West; & can talk with equal confidence on bridge-building in Alaska & the trappers of Northern Canada, though he started his career as engineer on a tramp steamer that pottered around India & the East. And one was in the neighbourhood of Lake Nyassa after ivory when war broke out. When a mail came in if I had nothing to read, I could choose between the "Grimsby Herald", the "Los Angeles Daily Times", the "Melbourne Weekly Chronicle" or the "Calcutta Advocate". When the Battalion was first raised, it must have been without doubt one of the most remarkable collections of men that ever was got together.

There were one or two other little things I was going to mention, particularly an account of the "Silent" Navy on the occasion of our expedition up the Lukuledi; but I will write to Gwyneth in a day or two instead.

Very best love to all from

Your affectionate son

Roland

P.S. I hope you didn't forget Norah's birthday.

~

The "Silent Navy" story in Letter 77 must refer to the action on June 10th-11th, 1917, at Ziwani, when the Fusiliers were towed at night by motor launch eight miles up the Lukuledi estuary. They landed in a swamp at the shore end of a railway, from which they made their way inland. By 7.30 a.m. they had covered 12 miles and come up against the main German position they had been sent to attack. They gradually advanced through dense bush, without returning fire, until they were within some 30 yards. Here they opened a "terrific fire", followed by a bayonet charge that caused the Germans to retire, abandoning stores, workshops and three machine guns. The 25th Royal Fusiliers suffered some 20 casualties.

∼

[No. 77 – returning health – wildlife – 'the Silent Navy']

No. 3 General Hospital
Durban
6th January 1918

My Dear Gwyneth,

I promised in a long letter I sent home the other day that I would write to you in a few days time. The probability is, I suppose, that this letter will arrive first & set you wondering what half of it is about, or, at best, both will arrive simultaneously; but as I have nothing much to do at the moment, I may as well get on with it.

I am still at Durban, though we have been daily expecting to go to Cape Town, where there is a hospital intended for Imperials – which the Durban Hospitals are not. I am afraid the journey will be by boat, which is a bore, as I would sooner go by train again. True, it will be by hospital boat, which should be comfortable enough, but I'm fed up with boats; & anyway it will be a pretty rough passage round the Cape. I am feeling pretty fit – have just had four eggs for breakfast, not to mention porridge. My favourite way of spending the afternoon is to go down to the West St. Hut, have a vegetable salad, bread, butter, a couple of eggs, some buttered scones & a fruit salad; & then get back home to tea.

I believe I said I would tell you a few more items of interest, but if I had some in mind I have quite forgotten what they were. Oh, one was to warn you not to expect any thrilling accounts of adventures with big game. I might almost have been on Tooting Common all the time for all the wild animals I saw. Lions used to roar at night round our camp at Mtama & also at Nyangao, but of course one never saw anything of them. Snakes up to about five feet in length were pretty plentiful, but nothing larger. Monkeys simply swarmed in many places, but mostly of a small variety. The Lukuledi was absolutely full of crocs – there was hardly a square foot of mud bank that didn't show spoor, but they generally lay pretty low, & only occasionally you spotted one floating like a log. There were some magnificent lizards – you can hardly imagine the size & colouring of them, & now & again we caught a chameleon & made him change colour till he was blue in the face. That, I think, is all I can say about animals. No doubt there were, or had been plenty in the district, but I don't suppose 5 inch howitzers in constant use & a few score machine guns were much inducement to them to stop there.

I was going to tell you why we are always willing to give the Navy their complimentary title of "the Silent Navy". One evening the whole Battalion embarked on a lighter & was towed up the river. We had spent the previous afternoon practising transferring from the lighter into small boats & disembarking without the least noise.

The orders were – no smoking (even down in the well of the lighter where it couldn't possibly be seen except from an aeroplane), no talking – perfect absolute silence. The scheme was to go up the river thus as far as possible; when boats from a Monitor[1] would meet us & take us up to the spot appointed for the "surprise" landing.

So we set off in the evening, & almost at once the tropical night descended, the banks of the river were blotted out & nothing remained to see, & little to hear except the churning of water by the screw of the tug. For two hours we glided silently up the dark streams; islands loomed up ahead, & dropped astern; sometimes we had to hug the bank to avoid shoals, sometimes out in mid-stream the banks vanished in the gloom. At length we reached the limit of navigation for our craft, came to anchor, & the silence was complete.

Presently out of the darkness ahead came the chug-chugging of a motor launch; & as it approached we perceived that every man on board was smoking a cigarette the tip of which seemed as brilliant as an arc lamp. Then the Silent Navy got to work. "LIGHTER A-H-O-O-Y" "SEVERN A-H-O-O-Y" "HOW MANY TROOPS ABOARD?" "ABOUT A HUNDRED & NINETY SIR" "TELL 'EM TO BE READY ON THE STARBOARD SIDE". Then came a little discussion about ropes, lashings, gang-planks, gentlemen's eyes, other people's whole appearance, ancestors & future careers, & other delightful topics, all conducted similarly sotto voce; & eventually we all managed to tumble somehow into small boats & continue our journey up stream, with the assistance of several launches, each towing two or three boats. But the water was getting low, & soon the Navy began to give us some more silence. "HI BILL" … "HI BILL" "HALLO" "I'M AGROUND", "GIVE US A TOW" "ALL RIGHT, HANG ON, WE'RE LANDING ABOUT HERE" "WHERE" "ABOUT A HUNDRED YARDS UP". And so we were; it was the "surprise" landing-place, & we jumped off into mud knee deep; but some of the boats were so firmly stuck they had to wait for the tide again; & it was near 3 in the morning before the "surprise" landing was un fait accompli. We did not get in touch with the Germans for five hours; during the greater part of which period we preserved complete silence. At 4 in the afternoon we drove them out of their positions, & the expedition proved a complete success – a success half of the credit for which is due, as we all agree, to the tact, initiative & devotion to duty of "our Silent Navy".

Best love to all from your affectionate brother

Roland

---

[1] *Monitor*: a shallow-draught warship, mounting powerful guns, which was normally used either for coastal defence or the bombardment of coastal positions. The monitors *Severn* and *Mersey* had originally been brought out to help deal with the German cruiser *Konigsberg*, which was destroyed at its refuge in the Rufigi delta in July 1915. The monitors remained in the theatre and provided artillery and logistical support for forces operating close to the major rivers in East Africa.

At the beginning of December 1917, of the 200 men who had been in Roland's company, only 17 had been able to march into camp at Lindi after their operations in the bush. Now finished as an effective unit, the 25th (Service) Battalion, Royal Fusiliers (Frontiersmen), left for England at the end of the year. It was finally disbanded on June 29th, 1918. The regimental history described the 25th Royal Fusiliers as a "romantic band of adventurers" who had won "great fame in the most trying campaign of the war".[1]

~

---

[1] H.C. O' Neill: "The Royal Fusiliers in the Great War", William Heinemann, 1922.

Chapter 9

CONCLUSION

Roland's letter of January 6th, 1918, is the last in the archive. It seems unlikely that such a dedicated letter-writer would have stopped writing home; however, like the letters that he must have written between August 1914 and May 1915, his later correspondence has not survived. Therefore, we know virtually nothing of Roland's remaining time in the Army. What is known is that, on his return home, he finally applied for a commission and that this was awarded in March 1919, shortly before his discharge from the Army.

On leaving the Army, Roland returned to the legal department of the Prudential. Here he would have been re-united with Claude Fryer, who had also survived the war and who went on to become a Deputy Controller at the Prudential. By the late 1920s, Roland was studying for his law examinations. Sadly, having survived the Western Front and the campaign in East Africa, he succumbed to cancer on May 2nd, 1930, at the age of 40. He died at the family home in Park Road, Coventry, with his step-mother, Sarah, at his bedside.

Roland is buried at the city's London Road Cemetery, next to his father, Joseph, who had died in 1928, and his mother, Hannah, who had died in 1893. Roland's step-mother, Sarah, lived on until 1951, surviving the bombing of Coventry, although forced to evacuate to Leamington. Of Roland's half-sisters, Hilda had died before him, in 1929. Gwyneth, to whom a number of Roland's letters were written, went on to work in banking and died in 1982. Norah, outlived all her siblings, dying shortly before her 96th birthday in 1998. She had devoted much of her early life to nursing the handicapped Phillip, who died in 1947. None of the Mountfort sisters married; by contrast, all of the brothers, with the exception of Roland and Phillip did so, and the present-day family is descended from them. The two sons of Joseph's first marriage, Louis and Vincent, lived until 1950 and 1966, respectively. Louis had pursued a successful career in civil engineering and Vincent had worked as a civil servant, employed at the Air Ministry at the time of his marriage in 1927. Roland's natural brother, Dormor, survived the Great War, and also went back to work in insurance; he married relatively late in life and died in 1962. Roland's half-brother, Geoffrey, also survived the war but subsequently left England to start a new life in Canada. Like other young ex-military men, he found satisfaction in the outdoor life of British Columbia, working as a surveyor and running a fishing-lodge. He died in British Columbia in 1984.

Neville Mountfort, Phillip's twin, was the last of Joseph's sons to attend King Henry VIII School. On leaving the School in 1922, he went at first into banking but subsequently pursued a career in the Midlands' motor industry. It was Neville who answered Malcolm Brown's appeal for source material on the Battle of the Somme and entrusted the letters to the safekeeping of the Imperial War Museum (see Malcolm Brown's 'Preface').

Neville, who died in 1992, remembered Roland affectionately as: "unselfish, generous, cheerful and a delightful conversationalist, but inclined to be an intellectual snob!" It was these qualities, that Neville so valued, that have also ensured that Roland Mountfort left such a lively and engaging record of his experiences in the British Army during the Great War.

~

Appendix 1

MOUNTFORT FAMILY TREE

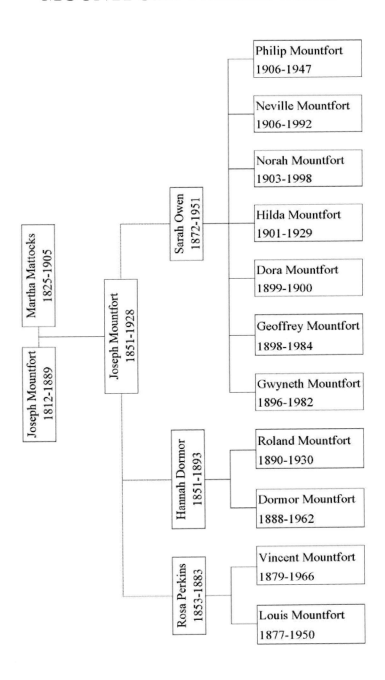

Appendix 2

ROLAND'S LITERARY TASTE

That Roland Mountfort found time during the duties and responsibilities of warfare to read as much as is documented in his letters, is in itself worthy of note; when one considers his choice of reading material it presents a fascinating picture of the man, and the times in which he lived. One presumes – perhaps condescendingly – that the conditions of war would not be conducive for the average Great War soldier immersing himself in the works of, say, Thackeray or Scott, no matter how much those earlier works might have been to his taste. One wonders how a Coventry man such as Mountfort would have responded, as a Midlander, to the writing of George Eliot or, indeed, to the plays of Shakespeare – we have just one, rather appropriate, reference to "Julius Caesar" in this collection, when he compares himself to the "lean and hungry" Cassius – but although we imagine that the literary education provided at King Henry VIII School would have been, at least, "solid", Mountfort's choice of reading gives an interesting picture of early twentieth century "middle England" taste.

Certainly, Roland refers, with knowledge and affection, to Dickens, Tennyson and to the Rubaiyat of Omar Khayyam: we have the impression of a well-read man who is discerning in his taste and impatient of anything which smacks too much of sentiment (he describes Bridges, for example, as "a wash-out"). He is a little suspicious of Oscar Wilde, whose "Picture of Dorian Gray" he calls "weird", and which he dismisses as "simply a clever novel". One imagines that he found "cleverness" distasteful; he also dislikes writing which preaches. His preference seems to be for a strong narrative, perhaps an adventure such as a Bret Harte short story, or a swashbuckler by Jeffery Farnol. What must interest the twenty-first century reader, however, is the number of references to writers whose day has come and gone: who, now, knows of "A Man's Man" by Ian Hay, "The Antagonists" by E. Temple Thurstow, or "Hushed Up" by William le Queux? Roland and his friends were particularly keen to get their hands on the many magazines which contained good short stories, or "humorous sketches" – perhaps just enough to entertain without too much of philosophy.

Roland is, nevertheless, a keen reader of poetry and expresses firm opinions about what he reads. He thinks highly of Brooke's "The Soldier", which, with its line "There's some corner of a foreign field that is for ever England" resonates more than many other poems from the Great War. Not for him, however, the Victorian sentiments of Newbolt: "There's a breathless hush in the close tonight…" would undoubtedly have rankled with a man who chose to eschew officer status.

There are occasions when Roland openly criticises the taste of others: he speaks of two solicitors "of rather aristocratic literary taste" and a Canadian barrister whose fondness for Gilbert and Sullivan nauseates him. His own preference, for a "sweet tale" or the amusement afforded by Walton's "The Compleat Angler", reveals a gentle sense of humour and a penchant for a kind of quiet, "English" reading matter. Though well-read in the classics, Roland Mountfort prefers the entertainment afforded by a good story-line and a poem with which he can empathise – and given his *own* story as revealed in these letters, this should hardly come as a surprise to us.

Sheila Woolf

Bibliography

ARTHUR, MAX: *"When This Bloody War Is Over: Soldiers' Songs of the First World War"*; Piatkus, 2001

BOISSEAU, H.E.: *"The Prudential Staff and the Great War"*; Prudential Assurance Company Ltd, 1938

BROPHY, JOHN & PARTRIDGE, ERIC: *"The Long Trail: Soldiers' Songs and Slang 1914-18"*; Sphere Books, 1969

BROWN, MALCOLM: *"Tommy Goes To War"*; Tempus Publications, 2004

BROWN, MALCOLM: *"The Imperial War Museum Book of the Somme"*; Pan Macmillan, 2002

BUCHANAN, CAPT. ANGUS: *"Three Years of War in East Africa"*; John Murray, 1919

CHAPMAN, GUY: *"A Passionate Prodigality"*; Ivor Nicholson & Watson, 1933

FARWELL, BYRON: *"The Great War in East Africa"*; W. W. Norton & Co, 1986

GLIDDON, GERALD: *"Somme 1916: A Battlefield Companion"*; Sutton Publishing, 2006

HOLLAND, CHRIS & PHILLIPS, ROB: *"Doing Its Part Nobly: Coventry's King Henry VIII School and the Great War"*; Plott Green Publications, 2005

HOLMES, RICHARD: *"Tommy: The British Soldier on the Western Front 1914-1918"*; Harper, 2005

JOHNSTON, J.A.: *"The Diary of a Rifleman"*; 1924 (Imperial War Museum 02/29/1 12383)

O'NEILL, H.C.: *"The Royal Fusiliers in the Great War"*; William Heinemann, 1922

PAICE, EDWARD: *"Tip and Run: The Untold Tragedy of the Great War in East Africa"*; Weidenfeld & Nicholson, 2007

WHITE, BRIG.-GEN. HON. ROBERT: *"Extracts from Diary"*; Richmond (Imperial War Museum 88/43)

General Index

163

Thematic Index